THE GOOD LIFE BOOK

A Professional's Guide to Happiness, Balance and Meaning

Brett Cowell

3824 Cedar Springs Rd, #1141
Dallas, TX, 75219

Copyright © 2017 by Brett Cowell

Total Life Complete™ is a trademark of Total Life Complete LLC. All other trademarks are the property of their respective owners.

The 5 Whys Technique was developed by Sakichi Toyoda/Toyota Motor Corporation.

No part of this book may be reproduced in any manner whatsoever without written permission, except in the case of brief quotations embodied in critical articles and reviews.

Edited by Jon Harrison
Interior Page Layout and Design by Yvonne Parks | PearCreative.ca

Published in the United States of America

Library of Congress Control Number: 2017900861
ISBN: 978-0-9976824-0-3

DEDICATION

This book is dedicated to my wife Darcy and to our children Jack and Charlotte. You help me to experience a good life every day.

For more resources and to join the mailing list please visit www.thegoodlifebook.com

TABLE OF CONTENTS

Acknowledgements	**1**
Introduction	**3**
Part One – Starting Your Good Life Journey	**13**
Chapter 1 – What Does Good Look Like	15
Chapter 2 – Understanding Who You Are	23
Chapter 3 – Knowing Where You Want To Go	41
Chapter 4 – Understanding Where You Are Now	49
Chapter 5 – Work/Life Balance Reimagined - Vocation	61
Chapter 6 – People	77
Chapter 7 – Health	85
Chapter 8 – Spirit	91
Chapter 9 – Expression	97
Chapter 10 – Summary And Quick Wins	103
Part Two – Staying On Track	**111**
Chapter 11 – Focusing on the Right Things in the Right Way	115
Chapter 12 – Nurturing Connection	135
Chapter 13 – Finding Courage	155
Chapter 14 – Maintaining A Sense Of Humour	169
Chapter 15 – Making A Larger Contribution	171
Part Three – Getting There	**185**
Chapter 16 – Taking Action	187
Chapter 17 – Getting REAL	201
Chapter 18—Planning, Doing, Reviewing	207
Chapter 19 – Place	229
Conclusion	**231**
Index	**235**

ACKNOWLEDGEMENTS

The task of a writer can seem a largely solitary one, yet this book wouldn't exist without the help of several individuals who've been both gracious and generous with their time. Rory Delaney and Scott McClure have been the most patient first readers. Thanks to Martin Cook for suggesting writing as an avenue to share my ideas. Jon Harrison helped me to generate lucid prose. Tom Lane was a champion with feedback on the exercises. Julian Brookes provided invaluable help with structure. Chris Fillebrown contributed his honest feedback. Thanks to Elizabeth Marshall for schooling me on how to refine and present an idea to a wider audience. Janica Smith did an exemplary job of managing the publishing process, and Yvonne Parks turned words on pages into a polished book. Thanks to Esther and the ladies of the library for providing a welcoming space to think and write. A shout out to the Storytelling and & Poetry group at Café Bohemia, and to such groups everywhere.

INTRODUCTION

All of us believe, at some level, that we have the potential to live a better life. Better in terms of happiness, balance, and meaning. Better in terms of our life making us *feel* alive, and allowing us to live without regrets. Better in terms of helping others and contributing to society.

Better for me meant walking the path that led to achieving my *true* potential in life. It took me 18 years and a near-death experience to finally get there, but now I've found that path. Trying to help others (and make the world a better place), is what I now do each and every day. I'm now also more like the father, the husband, and the friend I always wanted to be.

The mission of *The Good Life Book* is to provide you with actionable how-to material that can help you make significant changes in your life over the next 30 days. You already have all the answers to achieving a better life; you simply need to ask yourself the right questions. One of the most fundamental questions of all is: "What *is* a good life?" I want you to be able, with my help, to shortcut the process of living the life that you want to live, thereby minimizing the risk that you won't live your passions or purpose at all.

The first 11 years of my journey were spent traveling the world as an international management consultant, a job I'd once imagined having way back in high school. I strived and struggled to "climb the mountain" that was success in my field. I absorbed volumes of learning and got an MBA. I overcame obstacles and missteps until, finally, I reached my goal of being a successful globetrotting business executive. In three years I travelled to 25 countries for work, setting foot on six of the seven continents in the last year of the three.

Once I'd had this experience of success at work I began to drift, both professionally and personally. I pondered what was next in life. For the next seven years I tried to find a life for myself *beyond* the success I'd achieved. I gained a little self-insight. I got fitter and became more creative. I met and married the love of my life. I began an intellectual quest to understand the path of sustainable happiness and how to walk it in real life. In practice I was seeking a truly *good* life, and not just a successful one, even though I didn't yet frame it in those terms.

But life began to get in the way of a good life. My wife Darcy and I moved from the UK to the United States, and I started over again with a new team at work. Frequent travel took me away from Darcy and the type of family life that we wanted to have.

Then, shortly after the birth of our son, I had an experience that changed my life. Visiting my hometown of Sydney, Australia, I was caught in rough surf at a beach while bodysurfing. The waves tossed me over and over; I didn't know which way was up. My life literally flashed before my eyes. I wondered if this was the end. Then I felt the water receding and myself on all fours in the shallows with the sand and foam of the outgoing wave rushing all around me. The next day, at another beach, the experience came back to my mind as I was watching surfers catching waves in the light of the late afternoon sun. A moment of enlightenment came over me. I realized that the surfers came out, day after day, in all sorts of conditions to express themselves and pursue life, not to *chase* happiness. Surfing is a great metaphor for life (and for surfers it is a way of life). We must have the courage to paddle out and use our instinct and personal flair to achieve the best outcome to anything that life throws at us, rather than trying to somehow control the universe so that we can be happy.

Just over a year after that incident in the Australian surf, I quit my management consulting job to write the first edition of this book. In my head was the insight that I could use my consulting skills and mindset to accelerate the path to a good life for others. Despite the fear of doing so, *not* quitting my job became more painful than continuing to live life in a so-called comfort zone—a comfort zone where I wouldn't fulfill any deep purpose or live the type of life I yearned to live through helping others.

Over the past months since first publishing the book, I've found myself in a new and exciting yet somehow familiar position. I am again pursuing success, but this time from the starting point of my passions and values, and not just in the hope of living them. In the short time since *The Good Life Book* has been published I've been touched by stories of how the message and content of the book have already changed lives for the better. This feedback makes me feel certain that I'm on the right path.

My focus now is on bringing the message of a good life to the greatest number of people I can, and giving you, the reader, coaching and encouragement to believe in your ability and build a better life for yourself, and on your terms.

෴ ෴ ෴

The approach that you'll find detailed in this book is based on my almost 20 years of experience in helping people and organizations to change in a positive way. To improve your life you need to be able to:

- Create a future definition of what "good" looks like that is based on your values and passions, and then design a new life using a balanced set of attributes, i.e., work, people, health, spirit, and self-expression
- Be able to overcome internal obstacles to change which would otherwise prevent you from reaching your potential
- Consistently take action, in both structured and unstructured ways, to move toward the life that you want to live

The phrase, "The Good Life" has a very specific meaning in this book, one which has little to do with seeking *external* measures of success and pleasure in the hope of finding a happy, balanced, and meaningful life. That type of "outside-in" approach seldom delivers happiness, balance, or meaning in any ongoing way.

> *One of the biggest mistakes that we can make in trying to live a good life is to chase happiness, balance, and meaning individually as things, rather than treating them as outcomes of a life that we actively create.*

The word "good" as used here always refers to an *inside-out* perspective on life. We build success on our values, passions, and a definition of good based on intrinsic, *internal,* measures, which also align with timeless human qualities such as dignity, love, hope, and compassion.

This book was originally written with mid-career professionals and leaders in mind. I felt that I had sufficient experience, both personally and through many conversations with friends and colleagues, to know that a paradox existed within this group of highly educated and successful people. Often they weren't happy, balanced, or *meaning-full* in their lives. They did what they were educated to do and what they *could* do, rather than what they were passionate about (and perhaps also what would make a difference in the world). If I could coach and teach these leaders to lead *themselves* to a good life, so my reasoning went, then they could spread the message and philosophy of a good life to others through their own words and actions.

> *The promise of a good life is about more than just a shot at sustained personal happiness, balance, and meaning. It's about how we live as individuals and as a society.*

Since publishing the first edition, I've found that the heartfelt message and structured approach found in this book are valuable to other groups of people at various stages of their careers and lives:

- Those starting their careers who want to find meaningful work sooner rather than later, and build good habits early in their careers and lives
- Those who are already successful by traditional measures but seek to "dial up" the amount of happiness, balance, and meaning in their lives
- Those in career transition who want to take a second look at what they really want to do, as well as examine who they are as people beyond work and career
- Those approaching retirement and seeking to fill their next chapter with passion, wonder, contribution, and meaning

Whatever age and whatever situation you are in, the principles and approach outlined in this book can help you begin to live a better life.

Your path through this book will follow an arc of personal transformation: a journey that takes you from where you are now to a desirable future state. In personal coaching sessions related to this book I use what I call the ABC model (see the diagram below) to help clients track progress and actions against their original objectives.

The ABC model of personal transformation

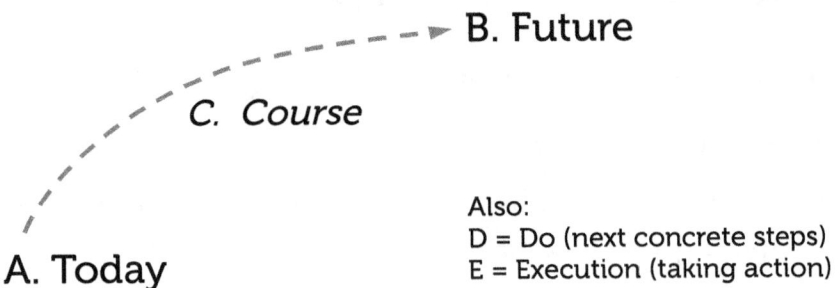

Also:
D = Do (next concrete steps)
E = Execution (taking action)

In the model, Point A is where you are today, Point B is where you want to be in the future, and C is the course of action that gets you there (additionally, when you use the model in practice, D is what you must *Do* in terms of the next concrete steps, and E refers to *Execution*, or taking action). Keep this model in mind as you progress through the book. I include the model as a bonus in this updated introduction because the ABC model can be used to shape your own transformation journey and to track progress. More information on the model can be found on *The Good Life Book* website (www.thegoodlifebook.com) under "Resources".

Too often our approach to goal setting revolves around *things* that we want to have, such as a promotion at work or a new house. We put all of our efforts and resourcefulness into achieving a single goal, only to find when we reach the goal that it doesn't deliver the life we want. In the ABC approach, Point B is the *life* we want to live, including *who* we want to be, and C is one of *many* possible paths that we can identify to get there.

We set a good quality destination, and reach it more consistently, by first understanding clearly where we are right now. This includes building self-insight into *who* we are in terms of our passions and values, and *feeling deeply* the benefits (the why) of the change *before* we start our journey. In any significant personal change the most formidable barriers are internal (within us) rather than external.

A note on the structure of this book.

Part One helps you to understand:

- Where you are now
- Where you want to be at both the summary (vision) and detailed (pillars/parts of life) levels
- Your personal "burning platform," which is the "why" or *compelling*

reason to act in order to move from Point A to Point B

Part Two of the book offers you pragmatic perspectives on how to overcome internal obstacles to change in order to unlock your potential.

Part Three of the book details different approaches to moving from Point A to Point B. Instead of a single giant leap, successful personal change usually is the result of resourcefulness, experimentation, and a series of incremental moves forward. Part Three describes three frameworks (REAL, DEEP and Plan, Do, Review) that you can use to take action to achieve a better life.

To make a change in your life you must begin to act, and to interact with others who can support your efforts to change. Resist the tendency to get bogged down in any section or chapter of the book. Go through the entire book first, and talk to others about the meaningful content you are reading. *The Good Life Book* website also provides additional inspiration (www.thegoodlifebook.com).

Think of *The Good Life Book* as being similar to the basic drills that a pro athlete does, day in and day out, throughout his or her career. Practice allows an athlete to deal automatically with the inevitable difficulties of competition (in a sense a metaphor for life) and enables his or her innate talent to come to the fore, so that he or she may *soar*. Most of us feel that we're getting the most out of life when we're growing. Given this, the desire and need to change will be with us throughout our lifespan. I want *The Good Life Book* to be a toolkit that you can dip into again and again over time.

After first publishing this book my journey was to build my company, Total Life Complete. Today, my circles (see Chapter 2) are laser-focused at the intersection of Art, Business, and Community, as is my company. Through Total Life Complete I offer experiences, content (including a podcast), and training based on the principles and tools in this book, aimed at helping you to feel truly alive, and to live a life that minimizes regrets.

This book is one part of an ecosystem of thoughts, audio, and video designed to be interesting, entertaining, and of value to you. Visit the book's website at www.thegoodlifebook.com for additional materials, tools, and templates. You can also sign up for the mailing list to receive regular updates and exclusive content, allowing our conversation to be ongoing. The podcast and information on upcoming events can be found at www.totallifecomplete.com

May your path in life be a good one! Now, let's start.

"We are all working hard,
but are we working
on the right things?"

- Brett Cowell

PART ONE

STARTING YOUR GOOD LIFE JOURNEY

CHAPTER 1
What Does 'Good' Look Like?

What is a good life?

Think for a moment. Try to picture a good life. What does it mean to you? What does it look like?

It might involve making a certain amount of money, or having a high-status job, or a big house. It might mean living in a pleasant environment or having access to enjoyable experiences. Being fit and healthy. Spending time with family. Working for a cause that's bigger than you. Growing spiritually. Everyone is different.

In writing this book I asked hundreds of professionals a variation of the question that opened this chapter. Depending on where we communicated and how long we had to talk, their answers to the question highlighted one or more of five themes or languages used to describe a good life. The longer we had to talk and the more neutral the environment (i.e., not in a work setting) the richer a perspective on the good life emerged.

The languages are:

- Attainment, i.e., what I have (job, house, possessions)
- Gratification, i.e., what I feel (pleasures, access to experiences)
- Importance, i.e., what I need (health, quality relationships)
- Meaning, i.e., what I stand for (beliefs and purpose)
- Being, i.e., what I am (living your values in everything you do)

In theory these languages are not mutually exclusive. We all seek a more meaningful and authentic life in our personal vision of who we are. Yet, in practice, in the messy reality of our busy existence, we tend to prioritize a much narrower definition of life—a definition focused on attainment and gratification, which sometimes goes against what is truly important for us and what we stand for.

Exercise 1.1–Which Languages Describe My Life?

In thinking about your vision of the good life, what language(s) came most naturally to your mind to describe a good life?

Do you relate to a certain language or languages over others? Which languages describe how you look at life in practice, right now?

There is no right or wrong answer to the question, and a good life should, and in fact must, be defined by you. It is clear, though, that whatever we focus on will become our life for better or worse. Many of you reading this now will, as I did, have a definition of success and perhaps happiness that is, in practice, based mainly on attainment and gratification.

Visually, this focus could be represented by an emphasis on Stages 1 & 2 of the diagram below, rather than on other ways of living.

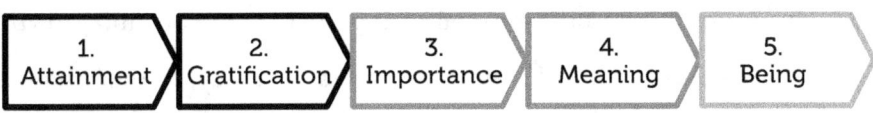

Figure 1.1 – Journey from Attainment to Being

My own good life journey led me to get more frequent glimpses of how the languages of importance, meaning, and being looked and felt. Those glimpses came before I started thinking of my life in such terms, and long before I changed my life to make importance, meaning, and being my default ways of living.

I could see clearly why I'd pursued the path of attainment and gratification and that the structures of my life (habits, viewpoints, beliefs) reinforced this way of living. I could see equally clearly why it didn't lead me to a good life, and in fact led me away from it.

We all try to make the best decisions in life based on whatever frame of reference we have at the time, as well as whatever opportunities are in front of us. For me, as part of a "transition" generation, going from a working class background to middle class life, I simply grabbed the best job I could find out of university. In those first years out of college I was still learning about myself and the world. I was trying to find love and to explore whatever came my way.

Nobody gave me (or gives any of us) a guidebook to the world of work. I had to learn the ropes as I went along, working hard and trying to learn from my mistakes. The five years between finishing my MBA and reaching my working definition of success were a rocket ship ride that was over in the blink of an eye. The ride was exhilarating and captivating, until one day it wasn't.

There are three reasons why attainment and gratification alone don't lead us to a good life. To get them we:

- Focus too narrowly on one area of life, e.g., work, at the expense

of the other areas necessary to live a balanced life (personal relationships, health, spirituality, personal expression, and growth)
- Use an external definition of success (money) rather than an internal one built on our personal values (integrity, helping others)
- Become self-focused, cutting us off from the timeless human qualities of love, hope, and compassion that we share with other people

The turning point in my journey through life, from focusing on success defined in terms of attainment and gratification to a more holistic state of living (being), came when I defined the good in life on my own terms, and based on what was truly important to me. Not that life changed overnight, but for the first time I had a reference point, a North Star that I could use to get my bearings and to understand how to get on track to a better life.

The definition of good I came up with and wrote down went beyond me to include helping others. As I began to take the first tentative steps toward aligning what I did with my definition of good, the amount of lasting personal significance I got from the way I invested my energy also went up. This is shown in the diagram below:

Figure 1.2 – Improved Significance

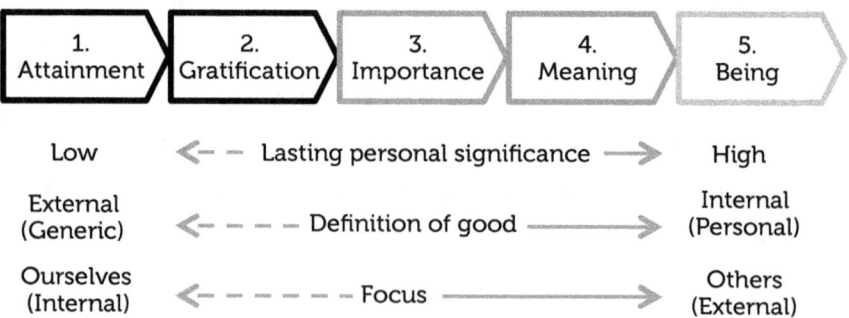

A key premise of any journey to a good life is that you must define "good" in your life yourself, based on what is truly important and meaningful to you, and aligned with your values. This will be the focus of the remainder of Part One.

WHAT DOES GOOD LOOK LIKE?

In consulting, we often ask the question, *what does good look like?* for two purposes.

The first is to help clarify the most critical outcomes of a project or strategy that we're working on with a client. This question is just open-ended enough to elicit the right type and level of feedback concerning what the project has to achieve in order to be a success (and how to measure that) without being distracted at this stage by unnecessary details concerning how the steps on a project will be performed.

Good could be an increase in revenue, or an increase in customer satisfaction, or even that the company is seen worldwide as a market leader in innovation. For individual managers involved in the project "good" could be a bigger team, a promotion and so on. For customers good might be that they gain access to a product that effectively solves a need or want that they have. Good exists on different levels. Good starts with an open-ended question and finishes with a better and shared understanding of specific outcomes and how they may be measured.

We can ask, *what does good look like?* with respect to our future vision of life, or about individual aspects of our life. In fact, this is the process that you'll use to create your detailed and personal definition of a good life.

What good looks like in a journey to a good life involves giving up the languages of Attainment and Gratification and switching to the languages of Importance, Meaning, and Being most of the time as you plan and live your life.

The second way in which the question *what does good look like?* is used in consulting is in terms of doing work to help an organization to understand role-modeling, or leading class practices or processes in their industry or in other large global organizations. Big organizations, like people, have problems with inertia. They keep doing what they've always done and become internally focused. As a result it becomes difficult for the organization (or a person) to know whether they could be getting better results from their efforts and resources by implementing new ideas and, if so, what those ideas are. In Chapters 5-9, you will have the opportunity to research and to add external role model practices and measures to your personal definition of good, for each key part/pillar of your life.

Each chapter in this book not only represents a step on your good life journey, but also describes an ability (one or more skills) that you can use to keep living a good life after your initial journey with the book is finished. The supporting abilities in each of the three parts of the book are grouped into an overall discipline for that part of the book. The disciplines are Directing Energy (Part One—represented by the Sun symbol), Unlocking Potential (Part Two—Water) and Enabling Growth (Part Three—Tree). The reason for having these disciplines is to bind the concepts together and to act as signposts to the philosophy that underlies the approach described in this book.

DIRECTING ENERGY

Managing time is an important factor in being able to implement the plans that you come up with, but it is not enough. Time is limited, but energy is potentially unlimited. As a professional you have significant resources at your disposal such as experience, knowledge, networks, the ability to communicate, and the ability to influence others. Your ability to marshal and direct these resources is a kind of energy that multiplies what you could achieve alone. Direct is a verb, implying action, i.e., the opposite of simply going with the flow. Hence the discipline/philosophy of Directing Energy.

Your personality and emotions are energy. For example, as the singer John Lydon has said, "Anger is an energy". Frustration that your life isn't the way you'd like it to be is an energy that can be used to move forward. *Hope* is energy. Your energy can be transmitted to others by what you say and do, and by how you live. To get the most out of life, don't reduce yourself to being a cog in a machine, with what you get being merely a result of time put in. The promise of a good life is working smarter, not harder. Do that by directing energy.

Many of us try to live a better life, taking as a given numerous real and imagined constraints, and thus not achieving what we seek from life, which leaves many of us feeling frustrated and perhaps resigned.

Instead we must create an *unconstrained* vision of the future, aligned with our values (see Part One). Then we rely on a *different* process, one focused on the *removal of obstacles* (Part Two) to achieving our potential, and then on *resourceful execution* (Part Three) of our vision in order to achieve it. Don't compromise your vision before you've even worked out how to reach it.

To start our journey to a good life successfully we must first orient ourselves. The next three chapters deal with who you are (self-insight), where you want to go (vision), and where you are now (your current situation).

Exercise 1.2– Starting Your Good Life Journey

Before moving on, take some time to reflect on what you've read so far. Where are you now in terms of focusing on attainment, gratification, importance, meaning, and being? What are your initial observations and impressions at the start of your good life journey?

Will you decide to try to live a good life?

NOTES

CHAPTER 2
Understanding Who You Are

Often we start our good life journey in a situation where how we spend our energy and time (what we do) doesn't align with our passions and core values (who we are). For example, we might feel that we have a "work self" and a "real self" that are different. Part of the approach to a good life is to reconcile these two selves, and to do this we must start with understanding who we are in terms of our real self.

This chapter contains four exercises that will help you to build insight into your passions, your past and how your future story can be created, based on *your* values and beliefs.

Exercise 2.1—The Three Circles

This exercise is one of the simplest and also most profound I've done. Its purpose is to help you to think through your passions, and to get your subconscious mind working towards them straight away.

I first did this exercise as part of an MBA class led by one of my favorite lecturers, Marcus Cohen. He said something like this: *To manage others successfully you need to know and manage yourself. My passions are business, travel, and teaching, and this job allows me to combine all of these interests and get paid for it. I'd probably do it for free, but don't tell the school this!*

In the exercise you will draw three intersecting circles, with each circle representing something you are passionate about. In the middle is an imaginary job description or activity that combines all three. These would be Marcus' circles:

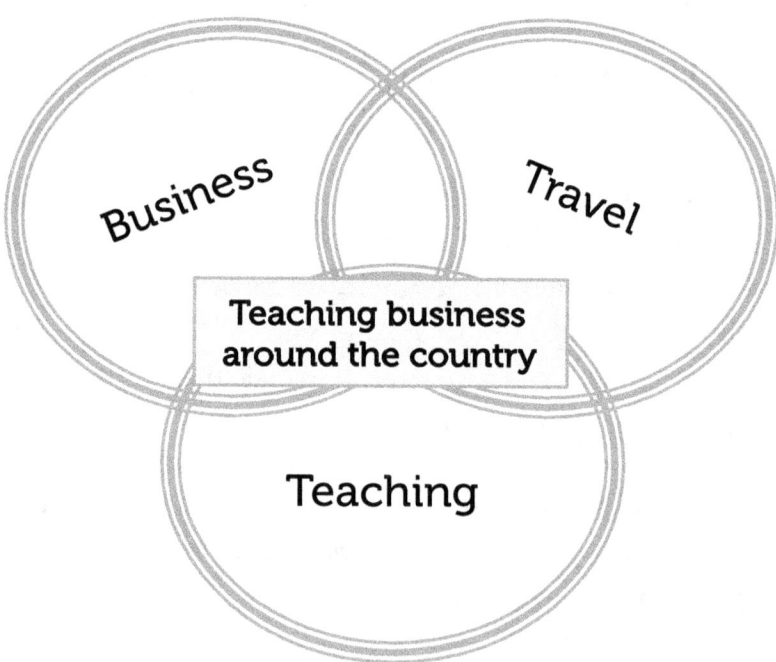

Figure 2.1 – Marcus' Three Circles

Now it's your turn.

Step 1—Draw three intersecting circles on a sheet of paper.

Your page should look something like this:

Figure 2.2 – Your Circles

Step 2—Write a word in each circle representing something you are passionate about, strongly interested in, or curious about. The word that you write should correspond to something that you love doing, something that you'd naturally want to do in your spare time, or at least talk about to someone at a party.

This could be anything from business to vintage cars to cooking or ending world hunger. They should be things that you wish could be a central part of your life, every day.

The purpose of the exercise is *vocational* rather than *vacational*: try to identify items that have longevity, not ones that are just exciting for a day or a week.

Step 3—Write a real or imaginary job description in the intersection of the circles that encompasses all of the elements in your circles.

Try to complete the exercise now. If you find that you have four or five circles then try to prioritize or combine what you have so that there are no more than three circles.

You may or may not be able to write the ideal job description *immediately*, but it's important that you try to now so that you give the task to your subconscious to ponder. You can return to it later if needed, with further insights.

The reason why I've asked you to try to write the job description is that it forces you to synthesize and prioritize what is important about each circle into a single activity.

You will be powerfully motivated to pursue this activity, since it pulls three of your passions together. As opposed to pursuing each circle independently, it is more likely that this single item has the power to change your life.

Given that many of us have limited time and energy, it can make sense to try to find one activity that maximizes the return on that time and energy, rather than try to carve out space for three or more. This is particularly important, since even if you select just one job description there will be many possible ways to engage in it.

Focusing on an area where your circles intersect allows you to go deeper into trying different ways to engage in that intersection, rather than having too broad a search area and ending up with just a list of three things that you like doing. Some of you may seek to make this your day job, or part of a vocational portfolio (Chapter 5) while for others the job description you come up with will become a defining characteristic of who you will be (outside of work) in the future.

When I first did this exercise I think that my imagined job was "travel writer" or something like that—which, if I'd thought about it more, should have been an alarm bell to someone starting an expensive MBA course! One night, years later, after a setback at work and while on a business trip to Istanbul, I found myself tossing and turning, unable to sleep (perhaps after one too many Turkish coffees at dinner). On went the light and I reached for the hotel notepad and pen on the bedside table, scrawling out the following:

Figure 2.3 – My Circles

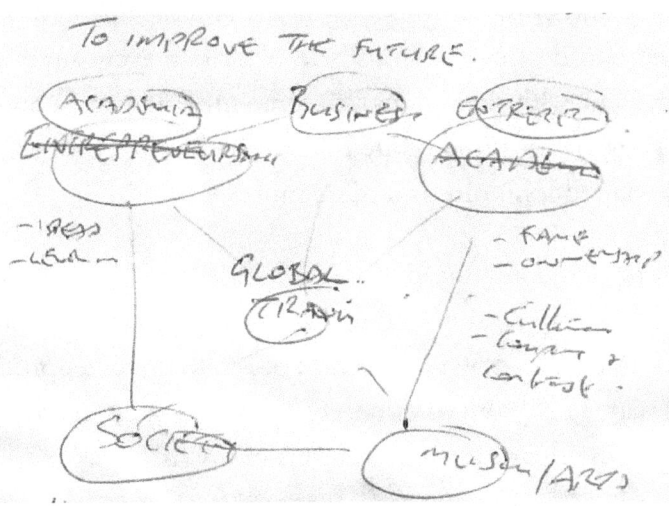

These areas are, clockwise from top center: Business, Entrepreneurship, Music/Arts, Society, Academia—with Global Travel in the middle. You'll notice that my circles don't exactly intersect (and, sadly, that cost me time later on). There was a job description or tagline that went with the circles as well, which was *To improve the future.*

Despite my angst about career direction, I could see that the consulting job I had did tick a number of the boxes: business, travel and even academia, which to me when I wrote it meant the process of creating and sharing ideas to improve people's lives—beyond, say, teaching at a university.

Since childhood I've had an almost genetic need to fix things that weren't working properly. The troubleshooting aspects of my job did push that button, but who or what was I really improving the future for? My interest in business had probably started with my Dad, who'd run several small ventures when I was growing up. The charismatic entrepreneur or leader had been the central character in the many business biographies and autobiographies I'd read at university.

Since moving from Sydney to London, I'd really been able to immerse myself in arts and music—from art galleries and the opera to the muddy, beer-soaked outdoor rock festivals held in Britain every summer. To me this engagement with the arts had become more than a hobby; it was a signal that my creative side wanted more freedom to roam than my job allowed. I wanted less noise and more music.

Within months of doing the exercise I rekindled my love of scuba diving, teaching, photography, and cycling. Doing so gave me enough of a feel-good boost to double-down on what I needed to do to get promoted the following year. This promotion demonstrated progress at work, but was it progress in the right direction in terms of my life?

After pursuing those activities, and almost one year to the day from when I did the circles, I met Darcy, the love of my life and the woman I'd marry. That could be a coincidence, but I don't think so. When you do things that you're passionate about and that let you express yourself honestly, then you grow and become a happier and more balanced person with meaning in your life. You learn to love yourself, a valuable prerequisite for others to do so.

With the benefit of hindsight I can see that I missed an opportunity to make a bigger and timelier life change with respect to altering my direction at work. I let myself off the hook on following up a business idea and dream. This was something that ended up happening anyway, but five years later and in a different country.

To have made the change sooner I would have needed to focus on prioritizing my circles so that there were three rather than six. The way to do this is to really understand what drives your passion in each circle, and we most often find that out through experiments and experience rather than more thinking. I've found that passions don't come neatly wrapped, and instead require tenacity to explore and pursue.

This type of tenacity is that of Thomas Edison, trying different approaches to pursuing your passion, rather than blindly pushing ahead on an approach that's not working, or simply giving up.

You can't predict the results you'll get from doing something differently, or from doing something you haven't done before at all. Before one does something new it's hard to understand the true nature of that thing. Also, one good thing often leads to another, unexpected thing

An idea that I'd initially resisted was to join a writers' group. I'd feared that I'd embarrass myself, or that I'd lose whatever made me unique. Yet it was only months after attending the first one that I realized that writing a book about my good life journey could be, for me, part and parcel of living a good life. The writing I presented at the group had nothing to do with this manuscript. It was creative writing in general. But the process of producing a personal expression of some kind each week, and trying to get better at it, gave me confidence and the feeling that I could imagine an idea and bring it to fruition outside the workplace. I also got to share some time with people who were in the same boat as me. The power of these two factors can't be underestimated when you are trying to grow.

Locating a writers group, writing a short piece and attending the first group probably only took 2-3 hours in total. If it hadn't worked out then I would've just lost a couple of hours. This is no big deal, compared to the sometimes weeks and years (or decades) we spend pondering where to start. It is perhaps ironic that I probably enjoy photography and music more than writing, yet it is writing that has allowed me to engage in both at a deeper level—by writing songs and through combining written and photographic messages.

Life changes are best undertaken by running small experiments, rather than being framed as all-or-nothing or "big-bang" type endeavors. Find out what works first, then scale up your level of emotional (and financial) investment.

The circles exercise is a great example of something that can benefit from others' input and feedback. Often it's easier to see the problems of others (and the solutions) with a clearer eye than we see our own, and other people will have specific suggestions or contacts that can be of use to you as you explore your circles.

Remember that often the best way to find out what your circles really mean in practice is through action. As a final step in the circles exercise, can you identify three activities that you can do over the next month to help clarify what the intersection of your circles means, and perhaps form the foundation of a future passion?

Often, being happy is not rocket science. Just know and do the things that you are passionate about and that make you happy for more than just a moment. On your journey to find the intersection of your circles don't forget to enjoy what makes you happy along the way.

Some of the best and most applicable lessons in life are those from your own past. The past often contains the seeds of future direction, as well as baggage that you must let go of.

The lifeline exercise helps you to visualize your path through life to this point, showing the most impactful highs and lows.

Exercise 2.2–Lifeline

Here is a simple example of what a completed lifeline could look like.

Figure 2.4 – Example Lifeline

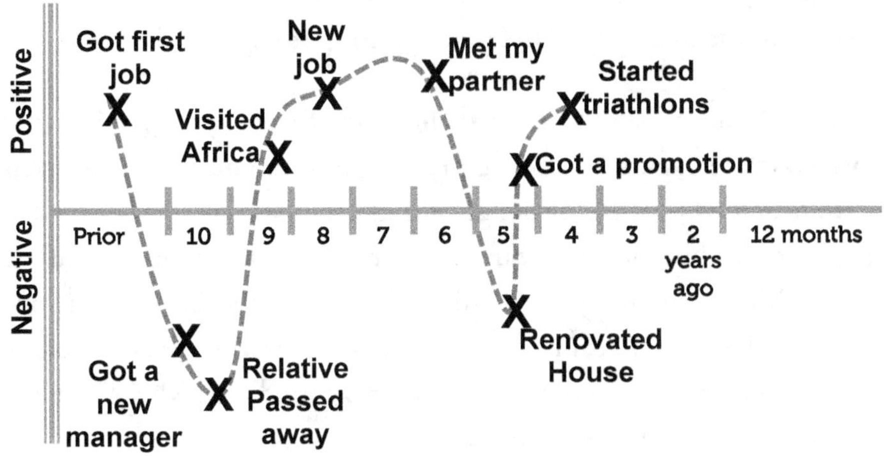

Here are the instructions to draw your own lifeline:

Step 1—On a piece of paper draw two axes that look like a "T" tipped on its left side, as in the diagram below:

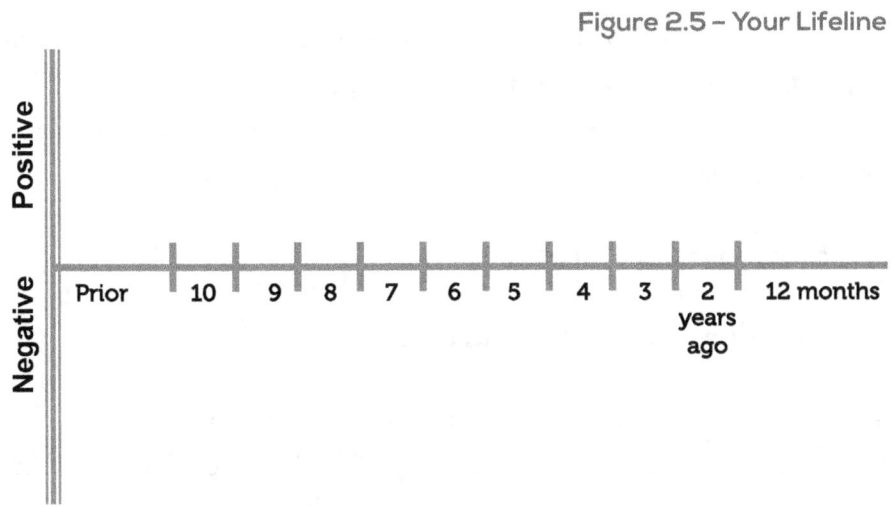

Figure 2.5 – Your Lifeline

The horizontal axis represents the years of your life counting backwards from the present. A typical resume will cover the past ten years in detail, with any earlier experience included only by exception. I suggest using the same ten-year period for your lifeline and creating a single additional column to capture any relevant life events that happened earlier. On the vertical axis you will plot the key events and turning points in your life, with positive events above the line and negative ones below. The further away from the line you go, the more positive or negative the event was.

Step 2—Make a list of key events in your life in an electronic format going back ten years, recording the year, month and day of the event, including how positive or negative that event was. Not every year will have an entry, but for some years and even months there may be multiple entries. Make sure that you record the key events that shaped you, such as a key job or relationship that changed your direction. What were the high and low points of your life during this period, and why? Where did you come from and where are you now?

Step 3—Plot the key events and turning points in your life, with positive events above the line and negative ones below. Remember, the further away from the line you go, the more positive or negative the event was.

Once you have the complete list of events, then choose the most important good and bad events and plot them on the diagram. When you've finished plotting the points then draw a line that joins all the points together.

Try to plot your lifeline now.

Step 4—Connecting lifeline and circles

Try to connect the dots between your lifeline and the circles exercise. Are there any commonalities or exclusions? What do the circles and lifeline say about your core values and beliefs (see next section)?

As with the circles exercise, you may find that you ponder the lifeline from time to time over a period of months, with further insights bringing it back to your attention.

CORE VALUES

Values are something that I've mentioned a number of times already, but our values are not something that we often consciously think about, although they have a profound impact on our experience of life.

The simplest way to think of values is as a personal code of conduct, a way to designate good and bad, and a means to interpret and shape our thoughts about the world.

To make this more tangible, here is a set of values mapped onto five categories (representing the Five Pillars which will be introduced in Chapter 5):

- **Vocation (includes work)**—Consistency, Learning, Providing, Tenacity, Status, Wealth, Money, Potential
- **People**—Trust, Integrity, Family, Friends/Friendship, Dependability, Love, Sacrifice, Punctuality
- **Spirit**—Faith, Peace, Humility, Hope, Solitude, Charity
- **Health**—Energy, Fitness, Clarity, Calm, Endurance
- **Expression**—Creativity, Openness, Experience, Balance, Growth
- **Other**—Wisdom

If your work and life are aligned with your most important values, you will feel at ease. Another way to describe the feeling of congruence with your values is in terms of authenticity or being energized. You can also use your values to give you clues about the work, activities, and hobbies that might suit you, and even the people that you will get on with best.

If the life that you're living is not aligned with your values, then you'll experience a feeling that ranges from a slight unease to a high level of anxiety.

To dig into your core values further, we'll do a short exercise on them.

Exercise 2.3–Core Values

Step 1—Start by creating a list of three bullet point answers under each of the following questions:

- What is most important to you in life?
- Which character traits do you most admire in others?
- What do you stand for (or wish you were able to stand for)?

Simply answer the questions above by listing three bullet points under each. If you list more than three bullets under each question, then prioritize your list before writing to include just your top three.

Step 2—Analyze your responses using the "5 whys" technique.

There is a powerful technique in operations improvement called the "5 whys". The technique is used to get at the often hidden, underlying cause or reason for something. Often, when first asked why we do something, we will come up with a superficial answer. If we're asked "why" again in regard to that superficial answer, then we'll give a slightly more insightful one. If you repeat that process five times the answers can sometimes be profound.

Let me illustrate this technique with a personal example, using one of my circles, Travel. I begin with a statement, then ask myself why that is really true. When I can come up with an answer to the question of why

I ask why again.

Statement: Travel makes me happy.

> Why? I get a new experience.
> Why? Because it takes me outside my comfort zone.
> Why? Because that is when I get to know myself and grow.
> Why? Because that is the key to reaching my potential.
> Why? Because reaching my potential is what life is all about.

As I said, this simple technique can sometimes yield really profound insights. In the example above you can see that my passion for travel links to a core value around realizing my potential and loving myself and others.

If I were to keep asking why, then this could be the result:

Why? Because that's what is required for me to love myself, and for others to love me, and for me to love.

Why? Because that is what life is all about.

You can see that after five whys the answers begin to become repetitive. A tip here is that although the technique is called the 5 whys, you can sometimes go to six or more. Through experience in using the 5 whys technique you'll know when you've gotten to the answer, and in most cases this happens after about (but no less than) five iterations of why.

Try to use the 5 whys technique to dig into your bullet point answers to the three questions now.

Step 3—Review your results.

Which values did you identify from the exercise?

Of these, which are most important to you?

Step 4 (optional)—Analyze the core values in your three circles and lifeline.

Try to use the 5 whys technique to analyze the underlying values behind the words in your three circles.

Next, review your lifeline activity. Pick three high and three low points in your lifeline and use the 5 whys technique to understand if those high and low points were caused at least in part by alignment or misalignment between the situation and your values.

For example, the values underlying my love of travel are wonder and awe, learning, and growth as a result of being pushed outside of my comfort zone.

Step 5—Consolidating your prioritized list of core values.

Based on the work you've done so far in this exercise and on the example core values that appeared earlier in the chapter, create a list of your top five values in priority order.

Although this exercise may seem like a lot of work, many of us spend our lives searching for meaning without looking for the clues that lie within our own values.

Character traits are values (and core beliefs) in action. We can often quickly identify good characteristics in others through observing personal behavior. Yet we also know that an ongoing situation (e.g., job) or habit can cause us to act in opposition to what we value. Our true personality doesn't shine through.

As you reflect on your core values, also think about which character traits you demonstrate (and are strengths) such as persistence, and which values you hold but don't often demonstrate (or demonstrate the opposite of), such as humanity or altruism or diversity at work. Your strengths identify a foundation that you can build a good life on, while undemonstrated values provide an opportunity to remove obstacles to living that life in an authentic way.

CORE BELIEFS

A core belief is a mental pattern, assumption, or truth that you hold about any aspect of life or society. We form core beliefs from our own personal experience or adopt them from our parents, those close to us, the media and the culture that we grow up in or live in. These core beliefs shape our approach to life, and how we interpret information from our own thoughts as well as from outside ourselves.

Often our core beliefs are a shorthand way of dealing with the world by automating how we make decisions or react to information. At other times our core beliefs can be wrong or unhelpful, forming an obstacle to living a good life.

Exercise 2.4–Core Beliefs

In this exercise you'll dig a little deeper, using the 5 whys approach to understand the core beliefs you have in each key area of life.

On a piece of paper or electronically try to answer the following questions.

- For me work is about . . . because . . .
- The role of people in my life is . . . because . . .
- The way I see health is . . . because . . .
- The significance of spirituality for me is . . . because . . .
- Growth and expressing myself is . . . because . . .

For each of the statements you come up with, please take the time to use the 5 whys technique to dig further into your response. Do you have positive or negative beliefs about each part of life? Do you think that these beliefs are helping you to live a good life?

Often an obstacle to living a good life is having limiting or wrong beliefs. For example, many people believe that work is a necessary evil that they'd give up at the first available opportunity. But is that really true? We'll look at the answer in Chapter 5.

Taking action and undertaking a difficult challenge are ways that help us understand who we are, and to *redefine* who we are as well (particularly in terms of how you actually live your life).

As you progress on your good life journey it can be useful to keep a journal or notes to record your thoughts and feelings concerning who you are and the progress that you are making. This helps with the change process, since it allows you to get thoughts and reflections out of your mind and onto paper. This is important, as you don't want to lose those insights. It will also allow you to group and synthesize the ideas that you come up with, and eventually to get to the stage where you have identified all of the major themes involved in understanding who you are.

Although we will continue to know ourselves more and more throughout our lives, it is not useful to have a permanent "work in progress" sign hanging over your sense of self. After a short period of reflection and insight (weeks) we must begin to firm up again the (new) view of who we are, so that we can have the confidence to move on with our journey and not get stuck in a cycle of self-reflection and rumination.

NOTES

CHAPTER 3
Knowing Where You Want To Go

It is important that we move briskly from understanding who we are to the process of setting overall direction on where we want to go *without* getting bogged down by the intricacies of our current situation (covered in the next chapter), the difficulties we may face along the way (Part Two), and exactly how to get there (Part Three).

Asking for what we really want is something that we seem to lose the ability to do as we transition to adulthood. An unconstrained vision has the power to make us sit up and think, "this is something I really need to do," and then tap into the amazing resourcefulness that we as humans possess. You wouldn't buy a new car hoping it has the same creaks and issues as your current one, so don't create a vision of a good life in that way. Unlike a car, however, your future life will be built upon your values, rather than how many dollars you have in your pocket today.

This chapter aims to delve further into where you want to go in your good life journey by considering passions and purpose, and by creating a personal vision.

PASSION

If you were able to write anything in the circles at all, then you've identified some potential passions, or at least some clues as to what your passions in life may be. Let's agree that life is better if we're able to engage with activities and things we're passionate about.

Although the intersection of your circles will form the "rocket ship" in your ability to break through towards living a good life, the rest of your passions and interests will provide the universe that the rocket ship exists in.

The next exercise provides an opportunity to document the universe of your passions and interests

A list of passions can be derived from your circles exercise and from the highpoints of your lifeline, and even from what you choose to talk about when you introduce yourself to others. Sometimes these passions are not fully formed, and we need to experiment with different ways to engage and clarify them. For example, one of my circles is *society* and a related value is altruism. Yet *society* is still such a very broad term.

There are many, many things that could fit under that heading that I would not necessarily be passionate about. For example, I don't mind volunteering, but I'd much rather do skills-based volunteering that uses my business skills to help charities, as opposed to painting a wall at a school.

An activity can tap into your passions in some circumstances but not others. I do like the process of purely creative writing. Writing a non-fiction piece with a definite purpose is different, since I'm more excited about what that writing helps me (and others) to achieve. In that situation writing is a means to an end rather than an end (passion) in itself.

Exercise 3.1—Your Potential Passions

For the sake of completeness, write down the longer list of potential passions or curiosity areas to explore later on. While you should continue to work through and revise your three circles, this longer list may provide inspiration for tools or enablers that allow you to explore your passions.

PURPOSE

One day, just before moving to Dallas, I was walking up Tower Bridge Road in London and had an epiphany that was like a voice in my head saying "there could be no better purpose in life than to help people who had lost all hope." The people that I had in mind at the time weren't the professionals that this book is aimed at, but those that find themselves on the outskirts of society, homeless or unable to put a meal on the table.

I realized that the fancy lifestyle that my consulting salary allowed me was actually making me unfit and unhappy. If I just stopped eating and drinking more than I needed to, my logic went, then I could just give the money that I spent on those activities to people who really needed it, and then we'd all be better off! In consulting we'd probably call that a win-win situation.

Perhaps because of my professional background (the skills I have and my identity at the time), the way I tried to reconcile this purpose and my own immediate needs was to set out to design a process to help others similar to me to experience insights into the good life, as I had. To use another overused term in business this would be called "leverage" or magnifying an action or resource to achieve a greater effect. I believe in the power of the thousands and millions of professionals in the world to effect a greater change than I alone can. Time will tell whether I made the right decision to dedicate my time to writing this book, rather than spending those same hours helping out at the nearest soup kitchen (in addition to the other charity work I was experimenting with), which would have been a more direct response to the insight that I had.

Like many aspects of a good life, your purpose may not come as the result of an intellectual process or even from searching for it. Instead, you may get one or more moments in which a topic or situation connects with something in your gut, your emotions or even your soul. This happened to me. Just as with your passions, working out what your purpose means in practice comes through practice, experimentation and being in tune with yourself.

I often say to people that to find the meaning of life you first have to explore meaning *in* life. A good place to start looking for meaning is the Five Pillars (Chapter 5). I know people whose reason to be on the planet can be articulated by one or a combination of the pillars. This process of exploration is not an academic exercise; instead you find meaning by engaging and acting in the pillars—all of the pillars—in a systematic way.

Often insights supporting a broader purpose will come from an extreme experience, either from a life event such as divorce, job loss, health issue, etc., or as a result of undertaking a difficult challenge that teaches you something about yourself. Purpose doesn't have to be grand, and it doesn't matter what other people think about your purpose. If family, for example, is your purpose in life, that's great!

VISION

Visualization is a technique that I believe most of us have heard about or used, and is almost mandatory for elite athletes, for example. A vision serves the same purpose but is broader, relating to our whole life rather than a specific event.

Creating a vision is simply a way to imagine a picture of the future before it happens. By doing this you can focus your conscious and subconscious mind to begin to make the vision become reality through your decisions and actions.

At the start of my consulting career I enjoyed listening to self-help gurus during my drive time to client sites. Quite often the focus of what I was asked to visualize were the *things* I really wanted in life. I was driving a Honda and visualized driving a Porsche. But is that a good life? This approach is half right. Visualization is a powerful way to make things real, but you need to focus on the right material for your visualization. Do I need to say again that, in my experience, money and things don't bring happiness? They don't *cause* unhappiness either, unless you sacrifice everything else to get them, including the time to know yourself and to work out what you stand for.

The most effective future vision is one that doesn't focus on things, i.e., "what I have" but instead on Importance, i.e., "what I need," Meaning, i.e., "what I stand for," and Being, i.e., "who I am." If you're able to build your vision or the story of your future life using the languages of Importance, Meaning, and Being then you're more likely to begin living a good life straight away, and only improve on that as your depth of focus and progress toward your vision grows.

My vision is:

To be location independent, and to be involved in a business that teaches and helps people to live better lives, and directly and indirectly helps those who have lost all hope, making the world a slightly better place, and giving back to the communities that I am part of. To have the ability to invest substantive time into being a good father, a good husband, and a good son, as well as a good friend to people who are and will continue to be my friends. I want my life to reflect an expression of who I am and what I stand for.

The power of a vision is in pointing you in a direction. A vision doesn't tell you every step of how to get to your desired future. A level of vagueness is essential in engaging your imagination and also allowing for resourcefulness in trying different paths and manifestations of your vision. At the same time, a vision shouldn't be so vague that when you wake up in the morning you can't tell whether you are on track or not. Before leaving my corporate consulting career the answer when I woke up in the morning, often at a business hotel away from my family, was that *no*, I wasn't on track. The specific feeling of angst created by this realization was at least better than a vague pain in my gut, or an overall numbness caused by living life on autopilot. Angst can be directed toward action.

The first step in making your vision real is to begin to identify a wide range of possible routes to that vision that you can explore further. You can use a set of decision criteria built upon the definitions of good you'll establish for your pillars to evaluate each of these possible routes.

You'll now do an exercise to draft your vision.

Exercise 3.2–Vision

Write a couple of paragraphs that sum up the key elements in the vision of a future life that you'd like to live. Be mindful of what languages, from Attainment to Being, that you use when you write up this vision, and of how the vision incorporates your passions and values. It may be awkward at first, but make a special effort to include elements of Importance, Meaning, and Being in your vision. To do this, think about what is truly most important in your life (what you need), and what are the sources of lasting meaning and significance that you've experienced or that will form the foundation of your future. What do you stand for? Which values will you clearly and subconsciously role model for others when they meet you for the first time?

As a reminder the languages are:

- Attainment, i.e., what I have (job, house, possessions)
- Gratification, i.e., what I feel (pleasures, access to experiences)
- Importance, i.e., what I need (health, quality relationships)
- Meaning, i.e., what I stand for (beliefs and purpose)
- Being, i.e., what I am (living your values in everything you do)

Write your draft vision now. You'll have an opportunity to revisit the vision later as you progress through the book.

NOTES

CHAPTER 4
Understanding Where You Are Now

In consulting I often found myself at the start of a project in discussions with a new client concerning whether it was necessary to look at how the current business operations worked and were performing before designing how things would be in future. Often the client would perceive that we should not spend any time looking at the present, because by definition they'd already thought that they needed to change. I share this experience here since I believe there is a strong parallel between why business change projects fail and why a journey to a good life may not succeed.

My advice in the situation above was always to create a baseline understanding of what is and what isn't working today, before starting on any significant change. For those areas not working (current problems) we also need to understand what was causing those problems and the impact of those problems now (on the organization, or on you in the case of personal change), and what the impact may be in future.

There are several reasons for this. You want to ensure that after the change you've actually solved the problems you set out to fix, and without breaking what was already working. Being clear on what the problems and opportunities are at the start allows you to have a laser-like focus in how you apply your effort—often a small change can get big results. Secondly, any change inevitably meets resistance, given the effort and resourcefulness required to overcome obstacles to that change. Knowing the impact of current problems and which future opportunities will be missed absent the change (often called a "burning platform") provides motivation to stick with the project and not give up when the going gets tough.

In this chapter you will complete a series of fairly short exercises that let you build up a picture of where you currently are in life.

Exercise 4.1–Current Life Score

As a simple exercise you will score your life on a scale from 1 (lowest) to 5 (highest) in terms of how happy, balanced, and meaningful your life is in each of five areas.

The areas are:

- Vocation (includes work)
- People (friends and family)
- Health
- Spirituality
- Expression (ability to express yourself and grow)

Give each area a score from 1 (lowest) to 5 (highest) in terms of how well things are going in that area of life. A score of 3 out of 5 means that you are relatively happy with how that part of your life is performing. If improvement is needed then score it 2 out of 5, and if you feel that an area of life is completely out of control then score it 1 out of 5. A score of 4 out of 5 means that this part of your life is going very well, and may not require additional focus to improve in the short term. A score of 5 means that this part of your life is something you see as a single defining characteristic of you (a single score of 5 with other areas of life being scored as 1's or 2's may however indicate an overemphasis on that area at the expense of others).

You can use the diagram below to mark your scores.

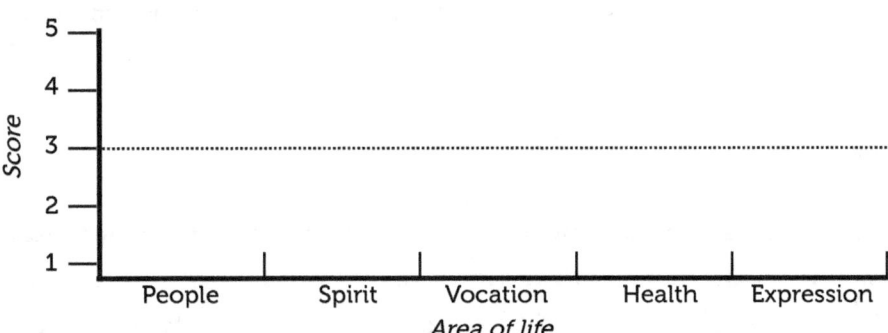

Figure 4.1 – Your Current Life Score

Next add up all of the scores and divide by five to calculate the average for all five. Although an average doesn't technically make sense, and in practice you feel the low scores specifically, an average can be an effective and visual way to see that you need to change, and to trigger action.

Some of us can easily assign a score to each part of life without much effort. Since there is no prescribed definition yet for each of the areas of life, others may struggle to assess how life is progressing at a detailed level.

If you are struggling a little, then discovering that is exactly the point of the exercise. How can we live a happy, balanced and meaningful life if we don't know what the right definition of good is for us? The good news is that in coming chapters you'll be led through a process to begin to define *good* for yourself. For each area of life you'll also define how you'll measure good, and actions that you could take to reach "good."

The aim of this book is to help you reach a score of at least 3 out of 5 for all of the dimensions of your life, and to maintain these over a period of time. Living a good life is about reaching a state in which each part of life supports the other, delivering better outcomes than if you were to simply try to "max out" one area at the expense of others. Once you become familiar with and comfortable working between different areas of life you will have a wonderful foundation to begin to further explore what your overall potential may be.

A different approach to looking at where we are now is to examine how we introduce ourselves. A personal introduction is a microcosm of how you see yourself, both now and in the future.

Exercise 4.2—Your Personal Story

Step 1—Imagine that you're about to attend a multi-day adventure and first-aid course with a group of professional people that you don't know. Since there will be some group work outdoors, and to break the ice, you and the other participants will be required to give a one-minute introduction on the first day.

Step 2—Write down the one-minute introduction that you'll use for the group.

Step 3—Analyze what you just wrote.

What are the main elements of the introduction that you created?

For many of us the introduction will begin with what we do for work, then something about our family and perhaps what we do for fun, or where we are from.

Did your introduction include any of the elements from your circles exercise? Why or why not? A trap that many of us fall into is to define ourselves by our job rather than what we're interested in or what we're good at. If we want to be more balanced and multi-dimensional, then our personal story should reflect that.

❧ ❧ ❧

Often we can believe that time and money are immovable constraints or blockers to our ability to live a good life. The next two exercises examine whether this is really true, and provide insight into how you use your time and money now.

Exercise 4.3—Time Audit

This exercise is really simple. For a week you will track your actual schedule in blocks of one hour from 6:00 a.m. (or waking time) to when you go to sleep each night. You may want to do this exercise electronically and in as much detail as you need to in order to be able to recall what you did when you come to analyze the results. I've found that when we're busy it can be difficult to remember what we did this morning, never mind last week. If you travel often for work you may also want to mark down the location you are at each day.

To analyze the results answer the following questions: What insights do you have after completing this exercise? Were there any surprises? Are there any "one-offs" that actually tend to disrupt your schedule on a regular basis? When does most of your work get done? When generally do you feel the most clarity and creativeness? Which activities do you *actually* do most often during those peak times?

All of us have times in our day or week when we are more or less productive. Any basic productivity system will tell you to focus on your most important work tasks first, and the seemingly urgent but actually unimportant tasks later on, if at all. *The Good Life Book* addition to that advice is to match your most important tasks *across all parts of your life* to the times when you have the most clarity and focus. If you don't you'll be living to work, rather than working to live.

For me, and I think a lot of us, the peak time for big ideas is the morning, specifically the first hour or two after I wake up. But what do many of us do in this golden time? We check emails or watch the news. If I could credit any single productivity tip with changing my life then it would be reclaiming the time after I first wake up in the morning, and using it to give some quality thought to what is important in life. Initially this can prove difficult to do, either because of other habits and commitments, or not having ready access to a list of what is most important. The latter issue we will deal with in the remainder of Part One, and this will help with the former. You direct energy by creating a process in your life to keep what's most important at the forefront of your mind, including the next *concrete actions* related to those most important topics.

Humans have sophisticated and often subconscious means of trying to balance the experience of pleasure and pain in our day-to-day lives. *Offsetting* is when you perform an activity or make a purchase in one area of life mostly for the purpose of counteracting pain in another part of life. For example, you may go to the pub or on a shopping spree to deal with a bad day at work. Bizarrely, I once liked to order new books to offset the fact that I wasn't finding time to do any reading.

Before moving from your schedule to look at financials, can you find activities in your week whose main purpose is to make you feel better about your life, as opposed to the inherent enjoyment of the activity itself? In the past I've rued not having enough time to explore a business idea that I've had, but at the same time I had plenty of time for socializing and travel to "unwind". That is offsetting.

Go back through your time audit and find activities that are offsetting or low quality unwinding activities. How much time do you spend on these activities in a given week?

Our financial situation can seem like an immovable constraint until we dig a little further into it. Many of your expenses are actually the result of choices that can and would be altered if, for example, you lost your job. Many of us have experienced the situation in which our lifestyle increases to consume any of the pay raises that we may receive. By reviewing your financials you can hope to identify what is the smallest amount of money you need to live on. This number is often quite less than you might expect.

Knowing that number can allow you to worry less about money, and instead be more proactive about putting aside savings in case of job loss or the desire to pursue a life goal that will take you out of the workforce for a period of time.

Exercise 4.4–Financials

Step 1—Gather financial information.

For most of us this step is a simple matter of logging in to Internet banking and downloading our credit card transactions. Compile all of your expenses including mortgage, rent and other key expenses that you create. If your expenses are relatively steady, then a review period of a month is probably sufficient. If your expenses vary you may want to review them on a summary level but over a longer period of time, such as a year.

Step 2—Group spending into categories.

Group your expenditures into a small number of logical categories. For many of us this would include rent/mortgage, food, healthcare, non-reimbursable work or education expenses (including work clothing, commuting etc.), children, travel and entertainment (holidays and eating/drinking out), shopping and so on. This is not an accounting exercise to the precise dollar and cent. The choices revealed by the bigger picture pattern of your spending and which spending is truly mandatory, i.e., necessary to living, is what you want to understand.

Step 3—Analyze financial information.

Answer the following questions:

- If you lost your job tomorrow what is the minimum monthly "burn rate" of expenditure on essential items (housing, healthcare, education, etc.)?
- How much of your expenditure, if any, is actually offsetting, i.e., to make you feel better about your life?
- Of your biggest expenses, which could be reduced significantly if you made changes to your lifestyle expectations (i.e., through an adjustment of pride)?
- How many sources of income do you have?

Step 4—Draw conclusions.

How do you feel about your financial situation after doing this exercise?

What concrete actions do you need to take in order to align your financial situation to your vision of a good life?

One of the easiest quick wins that enables you to see new possibilities in your future is to begin to divert some of your discretionary dollars into an escape fund, *especially* if you don't know what it's for yet. Most of our jobs are much less secure than we believe, so having enough savings/assets to allow you to survive for 6-12 months is great for peace of mind, as well as in the eventuality that you decide to make a bigger life change.

The question about sources of income will be analyzed further in the next chapter. Often we fall into the trap of making a job our only source of income, then bemoan the lack of flexibility in how we live our lives. I certainly did. Often, unless we have a reason and plan to do something productive with our money, it will go towards the ever-expanding category of "lifestyle." Yet having a good lifestyle is often not the same as living a good life.

BURNING PLATFORM

The origin of the term "burning platform" is from a story about a worker on an offshore oil platform. The oil platform was on fire and he stood on its edge, faced with a dilemma. Should he succumb to certain death by staying on the platform, or possibly survive by leaping from the high platform into the uninviting water? He jumped (and survived).

In our own lives we sometimes fail to make decisions that are good for us because we're afraid to, or because we don't see that we're at a crossroads and risk drifting down the wrong path if a decision is not made. We often don't appreciate that not doing anything is in fact a decision (by default) to succumb to whatever fate may have in store for us (good or bad). To compel us to act when there is a tendency not to, we should compile evidence about the way our life is now, and may be in future, that supports the case for making a change.

A burning platform in the context of projects or personal change is the compelling reason to act (and the reason why doing nothing won't work).

The location of your burning platform may be revealed by the life scores exercise that you just did. Is something at work, with friends and family, or health driving you to want to undertake a good life journey? You might find that your burning platform is a feeling that your life is not authentic, is devoid of meaning, or a realization that your life doesn't contain the things you are most passionate about.

My burning platform came from a combination of personal and societal issues. I could foresee that if I did nothing, family pressures due to work and travel would continue to increase, and my fitness level would decline. I could see that within a year or two consulting would seem like all that I could do with my life. The imminent birth of a second child would only heighten the perceived risk of deviating from my current track.

There seemed to be a lack of influential voices and strong leadership directed toward moving society in the direction of timeless human love, hope, and compassion, and away from materialism, fear, and hate. The solution to this and to my personal issues seemed inextricably linked and based around the idea of a good life.

What is your burning platform?

Exercise 4.5–Your Burning Platform

Step 1—Benefits of a good life.

List the benefits of deciding to live a good life, and then actually doing it. Try to be as specific as possible. How will your life, the lives of those close to you, and even the broader community be better because of your pursuit of a good life?

Step 2—Consequences of not living a good life.

- What if you don't decide and act on living a good life?
- What existing problems in your life will remain unresolved or get worse?
- How will your potential for the rest of your time on the planet diminish?
- Can you be the person that you want to be without trying to live a good life?

Step 3—Capturing your burning platform statement.

Write a short paragraph that addresses the question, "I am pursuing a good life because . . ."

Congratulations on starting your journey to a good life! The next five chapters help you to further define and refine a good life for yourself, using the Five Pillars framework. Remember to resist the tendency to get bogged down in any one or more of these chapters. Prioritize the areas that you believe will deliver the most benefit to you based on Exercise 4.1. Go through the entire book first, and talk to others about the meaningful content you are reading. *The Good Life Book* website also provides additional guidance and resources (www.thegoodlifebook.com).

NOTES

CHAPTER 5
Work/Life Balance Reimagined: Vocation

Often I think that we get the concept of balance all wrong, equating it with the idea of work/life balance. Using that approach in my consulting career, I'd ask myself: "If I'm working 80 hours a week, what sort of life can I cram into the remaining time"? That is a survival approach, not a good life.

Instead of work/life balance we should think of balance in terms of *all* the important aspects of life that we need to manage in order to live a good life, and that we would like to enjoy. A better definition of balance is a *multi-dimensional* life that is aligned with our values and personal vision.

From my experience I find that looking at your life in five categories works the best. The categories are meaningful work (Vocation), personal relationships (People), physical and mental fitness (Health), spirituality, faith and connection (Spirit) and, finally, activities that allow us to express ourselves and grow (Expression).

These categories are built on a foundation of our values and beliefs, and thus provide support for reaching our definition of a good life. For that reason I call these life categories, The Five Pillars.

Here is a diagram of The Five Pillars.

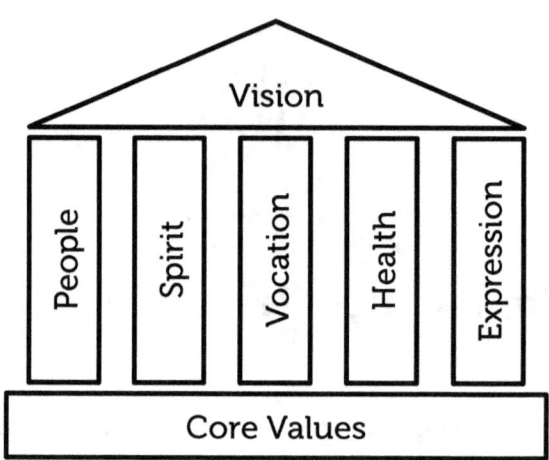

Figure 5.1 – The Five Pillars

To help understand which areas of life each pillar covers, here is a more detailed description of each of the pillars:

- **People**—Personal relationships with family, friends and co-workers
- **Spirit**—Spirituality, faith, religion, connection beyond yourself
- **Vocation**—Meaningful work, financial management, activities in which you use your skills to create financial and non-financial value
- **Health**—Physical and mental fitness, eating and sleeping well, and so on
- **Expression**—Activities in which you *create* the outcome and the outcome extends beyond yourself, e.g., arts, sports, teaching, larger contributions—more so than activities in which you

consume content (e.g., screen time). Activities that enable you to express yourself and grow.

To give you a preview of what is to come, you will use The Five Pillars as topic areas to set up your personal vision, goals, and measures as well as to identify the decisions, experiences, experiments, and projects that you need in order to get there.

Although it may seem more difficult to balance five pillars rather than two things (work and life), the opposite is most often true. Being specific allows us to direct our energy more precisely and in a proactive way to areas that really matter, rather than constantly feeling that we are reacting to whatever crisis a day brings. The Five Pillars can provide an effective picture of the destination that awaits you at the end of your current good life journey.

Let's jump straight into The Five Pillars by taking a look at Vocation.

THE VOCATION PILLAR

Many of you will begin the journey into the good life from the point of view of some sort of life balance problem. That is the reason that I've chosen to start with the Vocation pillar. However, that is not to say that it is any more important than the other pillars in contributing to a good life.

This pillar is not called "Work" for good reason. If the journey to a good life requires the identification and removal of false constraints, then associations with the word *work* can quite possibly be the single area where most of those imaginary constraints lie.

First, let me ask you, why do you work?

Most people will say "to earn money" or "because I have to" in response to this question, but for many of us work delivers a set of tangible and intangible benefits of which money is only one. For example, many of us get from work a sense of purpose, challenge, social interaction, travel, status, identity, and so on.

If work were purely about money, then it would follow that we'd always move to another job for 5% more pay if presented with an opportunity to do so. Yet in most cases most of us wouldn't actually do that, unless there was also an existing issue, e.g., a difficult boss. In fact, from the hundreds of people I spoke with on my quest I found that there are many who would take a 10%, 20%, or more pay *cut* in order to do work that is more meaningful, more flexible or has other intangible aspects such as working with a fun and friendly team.

In my experience the reason that many people don't make a move is a combination of their beliefs about work, their self-concept or identity, and the "friction" inherent in the way that the job market works. Sometimes this is due to a ratcheted-up lifestyle or severe offsetting that ties their finances in knots. Let's look at beliefs, self-concept, and friction in a bit more detail now.

Beliefs. In Exercise 2.4 about core beliefs and at the start of this chapter I asked you why you worked. It is common to have limiting beliefs about work, such as "if it were meant to be fun then it wouldn't be called work." If you do hold such a belief, then do you think it limits your chances of enjoying your work, or improves them? Do you think that this belief is really true for everyone? We shouldn't limit our vision of life and work to the single job or business we are engaged in today,

Self-concept. A job makes up a big part of how many of us define ourselves. Yet defining yourself by your job can limit your potential to live a good life. I will speak much about this in Part Two. One reason is that a professional role and network can limit the possibilities we see, and limit even more those possibilities that we actually, seriously entertain.

Friction. The job marketplace still has a high degree of friction, since it is arranged by title and job description, rather than by character traits or skills. There's no easy way for an employer seeking to fill a position to find you if you're currently in a different type of job, even though you may have fundamental skills, relationships, and character traits that would make you an ideal candidate for that opening. If you are an accountant and want to become a product designer, for example, this could seem like an impossible jump even though you may have several transferrable skills and a passion for creativity (remember, this is just a hypothetical example).

The solution, in my experience, to getting the most from the part of life represented by the Vocation pillar is to move your mind from the fixed notion of a job to the idea of a *vocational portfolio*. This idea applies whether you want to move forward in your current organization or industry, whether you want to change jobs, or if you wish to start a business.

A vocational portfolio is a broad *set* of activities in which, for each, you either earn a financial return or use your skills and interests to create financial and non-financial value. A simple example of a vocational portfolio would be to have a job, be on the board of a local school, write a blog, and have a property investment. Let me return to this example later.

There are several economic and sociological reasons why thinking of a portfolio rather than a job makes sense. Firstly, it's unlikely today that we'll have or want a job for life. Companies and industries continue to go through tough times and are more lean—meaning that jobs, including professional ones, are less secure. This is particularly so with advances in cognitive computing and increases in the sophistication and "seamlessness" of outsourcing options in low-cost locales. None of the companies I ever worked with as clients were trying to hire more employees just for the sake of it.

We are also living longer, so the idea of working hard and then taking a break before you die no longer makes sense. Instead, with the average lifespan stretching into the eighties, and retirement in the sixties, professionals will seek, and need, to keep busy for personal and financial reasons in that final quarter of life. Our values also remain in a state of flux—the desire for meaning over money prevails amongst many working women and men of *all* ages.

The concept of a portfolio is common in financial circles as a method to manage risk and return. A vocational portfolio is a way to manage financial value, non-financial value, and risk toward the best returns in happiness, balance, and meaning, all in alignment with your values. Needless to say, Vocation in an important space in our lives to which we dedicate much of our life energy, time, and attention, and thus justifies a more systematic and robust approach to managing it.

Take the example I used above of a simple portfolio. Your job may be the primary source of money for you and your family. You may also have a secondary source of income from a property investment. Your role on the school board doesn't pay a significant (or perhaps any) salary, but allows you to engage in the local community and to play a greater role in shaping your children's environment. The blog may not currently pay anything, but allows you to write about aspects of your professional specialty, including esoteric niches that are of interest to you but that you aren't involved in as part of your day job.

The key, uniting thread through all four elements of the portfolio is that you treat them *like a job*, by which I mean you approach them *professionally*, using your skills, experience, and networks to get a return. If you are an accountant, then coaching the children's soccer team would not be part of a vocational portfolio unless you were doing it for a material amount of money, or wanted to make sports coaching a major part of your future vocation. Coaching may be something you really enjoy, though, and it could be an important part of your overall good life portfolio.

Let's look at how you could use the portfolio approach in three situations:

- To get more from your current job
- To move to another job
- To start a business and/or add assets to your portfolio

Current Job

For this example let's call a job a relationship and role with a company, profession, or industry.

There is a "law" in operations called The Pareto or 80/20 rule. It states that 80% of the results come from 20% of the inputs. For example, 80% of the sales come from only 20% of the total number of customers on your books. Although this is only a rule of thumb, it is valid in most cases.

This rule also applies to jobs—that it's only 20% of what you do that really makes an impact in your performance. The trick is that it's often not the 20% that you think it is, and perhaps not even the 20% you enjoy. The 20% has to be measured by the person receiving the value from you—a client, boss or even, in a personal context, your life partner. Find out what that 20% is by asking them!

To help with the process of tracking value it can be useful to deconstruct what you do into groups of skills. For example, my former job as a management consultant included the following groups of skills: management of client relationships and sales; project management; company, market and industry analysis; creation of compelling oral and written communications; application of specialty knowledge in strategy and supply chain and operations to resolve issues in client's businesses; internal business administration and so on.

In that job the 20% that my bosses really valued was a thing called "management of client relationships and sales." The challenge is that what I liked the most was a different 20% called "application of specialty knowledge." What I really enjoyed at work was problem-solving with clients in the field.

To get more from your current job, it pays to try to find the intersection between what you value and what your boss values. You must also align expectations with what you'll focus on, so that everybody is satisfied and there are no surprises come performance review time. You may think this all sounds obvious, but how often do we work really, really hard, spending 80% of our time on the "wrong 20%" that is neither what we enjoy nor what the company values? If we're honest with ourselves, we have to admit that it happens all too often.

Another quick win for getting more out of work is to look for more ways to *contribute*. This could be as simple as becoming a mentor to other staff, or training others in your area of expertise.

Outside the company walls it's possible to use your core skills to do skills-based volunteering. For example, I was able to find an opportunity to work with a local charity in London while I was based there, to use my problem-solving skills in its operations and for their users, who were small social businesses. For a small investment of time I doubled up my returns by doing something that I love and that also made a difference for others. As it turned out, although this wasn't why I did the charity work, the experience also introduced me to numerous other business contacts I wouldn't otherwise have encountered, and challenged me to apply my skills in different ways and to think differently.

Another way to share your knowledge is by posting on industry forums or presenting at conferences. Although none of these ideas is new, what is new is the approach of planning and executing these items as part of a portfolio. This provides a more objective view of which items need to be added or subtracted towards the goal of achieving a set of financial and non-financial returns.

Doing things that reach outside your company is great for building your personal brand, independent of the company. This doesn't have to be a secretive operation—rather, most companies recognize that it is of value for employees to have strong networks and visibility in the marketplace. And it's good for you, too.

You should use your knowledge of what you're passionate about at work, and how you add value to others, to craft your brand in an updated resume and social media profile, e.g., on LinkedIn®. You should do this even if you are not thinking about moving jobs, and do it periodically (at least every three months).

Part of the reason to do this is to ensure that you spend time proactively *on* your career rather than just *in* it. By this I mean trying to take as objective a view as possible on how effectively your career approach is helping to achieve both your career and overall life objectives. If you become clear on how you add value to the organization, then your ability to articulate that and remind others at the right time may have more effect at performance review time than toiling anonymously on yet another task in your inbox. You may also realize that your passions are diverging from what you are doing day to day—indicating the possible need for a change in direction. If you are contacted through your online profile about another job, this can also be a confidence boost and a quick way to benchmark salary and conditions elsewhere in the market.

This same systematic approach also applies to maintaining your network through simple measures such as sending an occasional message, remembering birthdays and other occasions and sharing a link to a strong or relevant article.

Application of Vocational Portfolio to Moving Jobs

Spending time *on* your career when you're in a job actually makes it easier to change jobs, too. By proactively keeping your experience and network up to date you can most easily use those resources to aid in your job search without ever having to visit a job website.

It's also true that when doing skills-based volunteering you get to stretch and use your skills in different ways and also to do things that aren't part of your job description at work, but can be done using your professional intuition and generic skills. For example, you may be an accountant helping a charity, but be asked to provide ideas for marketing or fundraising or operations.

Writing an article on an external website can challenge and build your skills too, as well as expanding your network, even if that network is related to a different job or industry. Today you can find Internet forums on every possible job and industry. Using these forums makes it easier to learn more about the inner workings of different jobs and industries and to network online with other professionals—and even, in some cases, begin to build your own reputation by publishing articles and writing thoughtful comments on others' articles.

A little research and deconstructing the skills of the job you seek to move to is a way to assess any gap in skills between the two jobs that you will need to bridge.

For example, *accountant* and *product designer* may seem like jobs that are poles apart. Yet these jobs actually share a number of core skills such as: project management, ability to meet deadlines, a degree of customer service, professionalism, and the ability to apply a set of principles to create an output that meets strict requirements. It has been my experience that quite a number of former members of the armed forces make their way into management consulting based on transferrable core skills and character traits such as ability to work under pressure, a structured approach to work, and leadership skills.

Starting a Business

In the context of a vocational portfolio the point I'd like to make is that even though you may not consider yourself an entrepreneur, you can use entrepreneurial thinking to enhance what is in your portfolio.

For professionals it is increasingly possible to make money by selling intellectual assets (articles, guides, e-books, methodologies, courses) online. Could the creation of an intellectual asset be a useful addition to your portfolio? Scanning online forums is an easy way to understand the common problems and support needed by a specific customer or client niche. There are also a number of sites that enable professionals to freelance online for specific jobs or briefs. You may take this a step further to set up your own site and coordinate these jobs with several of your colleagues.

If you do decide to start a business, that also is easier than ever, given that it's possible to mock up a company website and to get feedback on what is often called a basic minimum viable product (MVP) or limited functionality version of a service or product without ever having to leave your desk.

This has been an altogether too quick run through of some possibilities of how to think about and approach the world of work differently. I implore you, when you sit down to design your vocation and your life, don't be limited to doing what you've always done at work, and then expect a different result in life.

You'll now do an exercise to construct a vocational portfolio for yourself.

Exercise 5.1—Vocational Portfolio

How can you craft a vocational portfolio that allows you to maximize the returns from your skills, experience, relationships, passions and interests over time?

- What will your job(s) or business(es) be?
- What financial or property assets will be included?
- What intellectual assets will you create and earn an income from?
- What type of giving activity or activities will be in your portfolio?
- Who are the key people involved in each element of your portfolio? What will be required from them to make your vocational portfolio a success?

List the components that you'd like to include in your vocational portfolio (or at least would like to investigate further).

This chapter and each of the four remaining pillar chapters close with three short exercises to refine your vision and definition of good for the pillar, and to prioritize a list of actions.

An important element of my vision is to be location independent. This means that I don't always have to be in a specific place at a specific time to create financial value.

I've grown up and lived in different places, and thus have friends and family scattered around the globe that are an important part of my life. I'd like to provide my children with an international experience and allow them to see their dad in quality moments, and not just frustrated after a hard day at the office. Being location independent as a principle is, to me, also a yardstick for whether I'm achieving my potential. Have

I gotten the best result in terms of Vocation for how I want to live life overall?

Exercise 5.2–Vision for Vocation

Write a short paragraph that captures your vision for the Vocation pillar in the future. How and where will you be working in the future, and how will you use your skills, experience and networks to create financial and non-financial value for yourself and others?

Next you'll complete an exercise in which you document the definitions and measures of good as they apply to the Vocation pillar. Remember to take an unconstrained view—don't limit the amount of stretch you put into your definition of 3 out of 5 or higher scores, based on what is possible in your current job or business. Likewise, don't include items such as "win the lottery" in what good looks like, since that is not a goal that can usefully engage your subconscious mind in order to make it happen. Please add your own characteristics of what good is for the Vocation pillar. For example, it may be important to you to be able to present at conferences or have increased visibility and socialization outside your normal workplace. Add this to your description of the levels in the Vocation pillar.

Exercise 5.3–What Does Good Look Like?

Step 1—Identify key characteristics that drive your score.

Recall the score from 1-5 that you gave the Vocation pillar in the last chapter. What are the key characteristics of your current situation such as: amount of income, hours, sense of purpose, people, flexibility, potential for advancement, challenge, travel and so on that led you to assign that score?

Step 2—Understanding sensitivity.

This step will help you to understand which characteristics are the most important to you, and how much they'd have to either improve or worsen to affect your score.

Determine how these characteristics would change if you moved one mark up or down from where you are now. For example, if you scored 2 out of 5 for Vocation (potential for improvement) then what would have to change for that to increase to a score of 3 out of 5? What would have to get worse for it to drop to a score of 1 out of 5? What would have to be in place for you to score yourself as 5 out of 5?

For example, the key characteristics in my score are: work travel and flexibility. Frequent and unpredictable work travel negatively affects my score, while more flexibility improves it. There are also certain non-negotiable characteristics. I'd expect whatever I do in the Vocation pillar to be challenging and meaningful, and at least provide a minimum amount of income to support my family.

Which characteristics of Vocation are most important to you, such if they improved or worsened it would have a dramatic effect on your score and your life? What are your non-negotiables?

Step 3—Descriptions for good.

In this step you'll write a description for each score from 1 out of 5 to 5 out of 5 for the Vocation pillar.

For example, my definition for Vocation 3 out of 5 is: working autonomously alongside a small and quality team. Some work travel (not every week). Applying specialized knowledge to solve problems and improve business and make a contribution to society. Flexibility to travel and take vacation in line with plans to visit friends and relatives. Flexibility to pursue a giving activity in my vocational portfolio. Income to support my family (quality but not extravagant healthcare, education, and living space).

The key characteristics that would have to change to move my score to 4 out of 5 are: being location independent for 50% of the year and having 30% of my income come from non-hours-based services (e.g., from intellectual assets).

My score for Vocation would be reduced if it involved a high proportion of work travel away from home, or because of reduced flexibility of vocation or ability to sustain giving activities in my vocational portfolio.

It is rare that you'll be able to complete all of the descriptions in one shot. Rather, you'll probably have to iterate through the descriptions several times to fine-tune your self-understanding of what is really important to you. This calibration process may lead you to change your current score for the pillar. That is okay! Just remember to resist the temptation to over-score yourself (assigning only scores from 3 out of 5 to 5 out of 5). If anything, it's better to score yourself lower rather than higher, since that leaves room for improvement.

For each level from 1-5 write a short sentence or paragraph that describes that level and any key measures that apply.

Step 4—Add external role model practices and measures.

If you haven't already, then take the time to perform some informal research on good practices undertaken by others in relation to Vocation. For example, many senior executives have a policy of not travelling for work on weekends, enabling them to be home with family.

You can find these examples through Internet research, speaking with your colleagues, or by reading about or speaking with those leaders whom you respect. You might also wish to find out more about location independence or portfolio approaches to work.

Exercise 5.4—Actions For Vocation Pillar

For the final exercise in this chapter, compile a list of actions and next steps.

You can use the following questions as prompts to build your list of actions:

- Are there any obvious next steps from your analysis of where you are now and where you want to be for Vocation?
- Is there anything that you've read about in the introduction to this chapter that has piqued your interest and that you'd like to find out more about?
- When you deconstruct your job or your interests, what are the key features that really make them interesting, that you are skilled at or are in demand by others?
- How could you speak to someone this week that could provide you with valuable feedback on how to move forward with your ideas on Vocation?

Record your list of observations and actions now.

The detailed pillar chapters that follow use the same approach as this one. Some readers might prefer to complete Chapters 6-9 in a rapid fashion and then "loop back" to their priority chapters after completing the summary in Chapter 10. To follow this accelerated path, read the introduction to each chapter and complete the vision paragraph exercise before moving on to the next chapter.

CHAPTER 6
People

When I think back on my corporate consulting career and my life, it is the people who stand out. At work the camaraderie built around working under pressure with colleagues and clients and in different parts of the world was hard to beat. Outside of work I'm fortunate to have a loving wife, family, and friends. Yet it is this second group of people who seem to have borne the brunt of the sacrifices of time and energy I made for the purpose of completing my work.

This situation is quite typical of the challenges faced by busy professionals: structured and sometimes unlimited demands of work overwhelm the unstructured demands of the people most important to them. Until there is a crisis.

A way to get better results from the People pillar is to use a more structured approach to how you engage with people. In consulting and project management we use a technique called *stakeholder management* to ensure that people critical to the overall success of the project are managed properly and effectively. A stakeholder is anyone who is materially affected by what you are planning to do, and who can materially affect the success of what you're planning to do either directly or indirectly.

In life we have stakeholders at home, at work, and outside of work.

The stakeholder management technique works through a process of *awareness, tailored response,* and *monitoring.*

Awareness

The first principle of stakeholder management is awareness. Who are the key people in your life, what do they need from you, and how do they want it (and how often)?

Stakeholder management is performed from two perspectives. The first perspective is from the point of view of the person impacted by your life and the decisions you make. You try to put yourself in their shoes first. Once you have tried to understand the world from your stakeholder's perspective, you then try to integrate that perspective with your own.

In the previous chapter I talked about the Pareto or 80/20 rule with respect to your boss, customer, or partner. What I was actually talking about was stakeholder management for each of those key relationships. We're dealing with stakeholders all the time, but often not in a structured way—a way that gives them what they need when they need it.

You perform the awareness step in stakeholder management by listing and prioritizing your key stakeholders both outside of and at work, then finding out what they want from you and how they want it. The next step is tailored response.

Tailored Response

Tailored response is simply adapting how you interact with that person to give them what they want, how and when they want it. Do your stakeholders prefer email, phone, or in-person communication, how often, and how detailed? What will make them feel valued, heard, and *special*?

In most cases *quality* is more important than *quantity* in stakeholder management, Giving someone a little of what they need is much better than a whole lot of what they don't want or need. You can probably think of many examples from your own life when you have been the giver or receiver in such situations.

Monitoring

Stakeholder management is not a one-shot exercise. Instead, you must regularly update your list of stakeholders, their prioritization and what they need from you (attention, validation, etc.), how and when. Sometimes you try something and it doesn't work as expected, so ongoing communication is important with your stakeholders, not only in the relationship but *on* the relationship, too (not just reacting to that person on a day-to-day basis, but taking the time to work out how they see the world and their underlying needs and wants).

Now let's consolidate this discussion with an exercise in which you build your stakeholder list. Although this exercise is introduced in the People pillar, it is applicable to everything that you'll do in your journey to a good life. You may want to keep a copy of your list in a place where it is easily accessible and update it as you revise the pillars and any projects or experiments that you may consider running.

Exercise 6.1—Stakeholder List

Write out a list of your key stakeholders. Who are the people that are both impacted by your life and also the most important to you? What do they need from you, how do they want it and how often? What is *their* definition of good for the relationship that they have with you?

Write out the list now, grouping by stakeholders at work, home, and in other parts of your life. You may want to put this on a spreadsheet for easy sorting and editing later on. Once you have the completed list you can also work out what you need from your relationship with each stakeholder and identify any gaps between what you and they need from the relationship.

It's ironic that we often give the majority of our quality energy and time to work, yet we say that people are the most important thing in our lives. Before I left my consulting job I was in the unenviable position of having further success at work mean more and more travel away from home and my family.

I'd established the measure of number of evening meals and bath times spent with my kids during the week. I was averaging two or perhaps three per week. On many work days I might not see my son at all, given that I'd leave for work before he was awake and get home after he'd gone to bed—if indeed I was waking and sleeping in the same city at all.

This travel situation was in truth bittersweet, as I actually enjoyed spending time in vibrant cities like New York and Miami, which I travelled to from Dallas for work. The enjoyment I got from certain travel, and from the sense of purpose and regular enough positive experience that work provided, probably delayed making the right overall life decision for me. I say this because more often than not we're presented with a life situation that is not clear-cut, but has both good and bad aspects. You may love your job, but the need to create an integrated life in which each component supports the others might force you to change how and potentially where you work. To resolve such a situation we have to first go through the exercise of being clear about the prioritization of different areas of life (pillars) and then be resourceful in trying different configurations to how we approach fulfilling our needs from each aspect of our life.

I had to face the fact that if I wanted to play a significant role in my children's lives, then something had to change. I needed to travel less frequently for work, and have the flexibility to find some quality time in each day to spend with them. This is another reason why the goal of being location independent (at least for a few years) is of such interest— as a means to spend more quality time with family. Beware here of your tendency to hold unproductive beliefs about work, such as that it must involve sacrificing your family. Must it?

When I speak with senior executives about the highs and lows of their careers this is one of their biggest regrets, i.e., sacrificing family time when their children most needed them. I wonder how many of these same executives have taken a lead to create more humane, flexible, and healthy workplaces.

The remainder of this chapter will follow the same structure as the review of the Vocation pillar. You'll first create a vision for People, then define what good looks like, and finally document a list of actions that you can take.

If you recall, people feature prominently in my vision, including:

- Teaching and helping people to live better lives
- Helping those who have lost all hope

- Giving back to communities that I am a part of
- Being a good father, husband and son
- Being a good friend, and maintaining a lifelong group of friends

Improving lives for people is certainly part of my value set, and no doubt I've spelled this out in my vision, probably as a reaction to working in corporate environments where process and profit most often come before people. Although the stakeholder management techniques you've read about in this chapter can be used to refer to individuals or groups in your community and wider society I recommend that you limit the People pillar to those in your immediate circle (i.e., specific individuals that are already part of your life). In my example above the people in my immediate circle are represented in the bottom two bullet points. Use the Expression pillar to list groups of people you seek to engage with as a part of an overall contribution to society. So in my example above the top three bullet points should be listed under the vision for the Expression pillar. The reason for this is to ensure that you always manage to focus on those people most important to you in the People pillar despite interacting with a broader group of people across all the pillars.

Exercise 6.2–Vision for People

Write a short paragraph that captures your vision for the People pillar. Who are the most important people in your life, and what will your relationship with them be in future?

Exercise 6.3–What Does Good Look Like?

Step 1—Identify key characteristics that drive your score.

Recall the score from 1-5 that you gave the People pillar in Chapter 4. What were the key characteristics, such as: amount and quality of time spent, relative strength of the relationship, degree of impact on you, on them, and so on that contributed to you assigning that score?

Step 2—Understanding sensitivity.

Determine how these characteristics would change if your score moved one mark up or down from where you are now, i.e., from 2 out of 5 to a score of 3, then 4.

Which are the most important characteristics for the People pillar? Have you identified any non-negotiables?

Step 3—Descriptions for good.

In this step you'll write a description for each score from 1 out of 5 to 5 out of 5 for the People pillar.

For example, my definition for People 3 out of 5 is: spending quality time every week with the people most important to me. The ability to not only be present in body, but to be able to contribute to and shape the lives of family and friends and others in a positive way.

The key characteristics that would have to change to move my score to 4 out of 5 are: the ability to influence those outside my immediate circle in the local community in a positive way (for example, a family friend runs a charity to help special needs children and their parents). To reach 5 out of 5 I'd like to be a role model to those close to me by extending my positive influence beyond my local community to professionals and others worldwide (through what I do and who I am).

My score for People would be reduced if I were not able to consistently spend quality time with family every week, or if I found myself rationalizing not being at home due to work commitments.

For each level from 1-5 write a short sentence or paragraph that describes that level and any key measures that apply.

Step 4—Add external role model practices and measures.

If you haven't already, then take the time to perform some informal research on good practices related to People that others are already applying. For example, what are the tips and tricks that others in your circle have for making people feel valued and special? Many of you have told me that you schedule time for people-related activities into your work calendar well in advance, and guard those with the same vigor you would for "work stuff that has to be done".

Exercise 6.4–Actions for People Pillar

Now make your list of actions relating to People. What can you do this week to make a difference to a key person or people in your life?

NOTES

CHAPTER 7
Health

If you've ever had the flu or sprained an ankle, then you know how directly and quickly a deterioration of physical health can affect the quality of your experience of life.

We are working longer and harder and our health is something, along with people, that we may sacrifice silently and with seemingly no consequences—until we face an emergency.

For the many ambitious workaholics among us the most important reason to focus on health is, at least sometimes, as a productivity tool. Managing health grows your physical and mental energy store, so that you can do more over a longer period of time.

Given that there is seemingly more work and fewer people to do it, many professionals that I've spoken to feel the need to be "on" constantly and operate at a level of peak performance, treating work like an elite athlete might approach an endurance race, and often with commensurate physical training. This type of performance training can also include techniques such as visualization and meditation, too (including micro-meditation and deliberate process switching of mental states).

What of the other half of the health equation, namely mental health?

Mental health issues like stress, anxiety and depression can, like physical issues, have a debilitating effect, and can sometimes be *more* debilitating, since the effects can come on more quickly and last for much longer. And not only you but those around you are affected by mental health issues.

Your perception of happiness, balance, and meaning in life is also heavily dependent on the management of your mental state over time, which in turn is influenced by the physical domain, including diet, sleep, and exercise.

For me there is no problem in the world that a pizza and a glass of wine or two can't fix. The problem with this approach occurs when you have lots of problems to solve. That's lots of pizzas and wine!

The way that I've made a step change in my health (admittedly from very unhealthy to moderately healthy) is to begin to cycle around a nearby lake in the morning. I also use the riding time to think about the problems on my mind. The time to drive to the lake from my house is around 20 minutes, and the routine to get ready and to drive there is automatic, not requiring any investment of mental energy. I don't read emails until after I've cycled. This means that I can keep my peak creative time in the morning clean for creative problem solving and new ideas.

When I'm on the road I exchange my cycle time for gym time at the hotel or a run. Given this productivity boost in the morning, I get more done in less time and am less likely to splurge at night. Instead of making the pizza the reward, I make the act of getting up to go for a bike ride a reward.

My lessons here are to find a kind of fitness that works for you in terms of both physical and mental health. I hate running but love cycling. I enjoyed learning Wing Chun Kung Fu in the past since it was "fitness with a purpose", just as others prefer to get their exercise playing team sports, given the social aspects. It's easy to believe that if you're out of shape, you're lazy. It may just be that you need to use your resourcefulness to identify the best kind of fitness for you. If you do that, then, miraculously, the lazy feeling goes away.

The second part to a focus on health is to look at your coping mechanisms for dealing with stress. When I lived in London I had a short ten-minute walk to and from the office along the Thames. This was a natural stress reliever. In Dallas that became a ten or so minute drive, which was not a stress reliever, so I made a point of trying to do a ten-minute walk around lunchtime, *especially* when I was actually much too busy to do so. Don't look for a complex and expensive solution to managing stress and regaining perspective; take a walk. Many artists, philosophers and political figures have made walks a regular part of their routine.

Despite the stress of raising children they can, in my experience, be wonderful stress relievers, too. I don't need to go to an expensive meditation retreat to regain perspective. I can get the same result by trying, for just ten minutes a day, to see the world through my two-year-old son's eyes. I also write bad poetry on my mobile phone.

Make the management of physical and mental health part of the discipline of life that you adopt and, more so, part of who you are. There are obvious interdependencies between Health and the other pillars. Ask yourself how you can be creative in managing your mental health through People, Spirit, and Creative or Expressive activities.

Exercise 7.1—Vision for Health

Write a short paragraph that captures your vision for the Health pillar. What will your future physical and mental health look and feel like? What practices will be a regular part of your life for managing your physical and mental health? What must you start doing, or stop doing? What does your future physical and mental health let you do or keep doing elsewhere in your life?

For me, having done the lifeline exercise, I've seen again and again that physical fitness is a precursor to the peak periods of positive life experience that I've experienced. In this way fitness is an enabler of life as much as a goal in itself. Right now, as I engage in the largely sedentary activity of writing this book, I try to ensure that I feel hungry at least once or twice during the time from waking up to going to bed. I enjoy food so much that I'd forgotten what it was really like to feel hungry. I also track my weight a couple of times a week, mainly to remind myself that I'm focusing on this area.

The number of times I take my son to play in the park per week is not something that I track as meticulously, but it is something that I'm vividly aware of, and by being fully *present* in family time (no smartphones allowed) I get to manage stress and spend some quality time with him. Life didn't used to be that way, so I'm grateful for the change.

Exercise 7.2—What Does Good Look Like?

Step 1—Identify key characteristics that drive your score.

Recall the score from 1-5 that you gave the Health pillar in Chapter 4. What are the key characteristics, such as: weight, how you look and feel, degree of or freedom from stress, anxiety, depression and so on that led you to assign that score?

Step 2—Understanding sensitivity.

Determine how these characteristics would change if your score moved one mark up or down from where you are now.

Which are the most important characteristics for the Health pillar? Have you identified any non-negotiables?

Step 3—Descriptions for good.

In this step you'll write a description for each score from 1 out of 5 to 5 out of 5 for the Health pillar.

For example, my definition for Health 3 out of 5 is: maintaining a healthy weight range and at least a maintenance level of exercise/fitness. Sleeping enough so that tiredness doesn't detract from my mental clarity or energy levels. Giving food treats their proper place—to add spice to what is fundamentally a sustainable and fairly healthy diet. Having at least ten minutes every day to reflect and/or express myself. Laughing at least once every day.

The key characteristics that would have to change to move my score to 4 out of 5 are: to consider physical and mental health a defining characteristic of myself. To reach 5 out of 5 I'd like to understand the field of physical and mental health well enough in a theoretical and practical way to credibly teach and help others.

My score for Health would be reduced if I were nearing the outer markers of my healthy weight range, and/or was regularly using food to feel good or to relieve stress.

For each level from 1-5 write a short sentence or paragraph that describes that level and any key measures that apply.

Step 4—Add external role model practices and measures.

What practices and measures are others using to improve their scores for health?

For example, at work I've seen that those who are successful in maintaining their health when on the road do a great job of treating their health routine as a firm constraint, e.g., asking others to move a meeting or pushing back breakfast or dinner time so that they can work out. Secondly, they co-opt others to join them for a morning or post-work exercise session.

Exercise 7.3–Actions for Health Pillar

Make your list of actions now relating to Health. What can you do this week to make a difference in your Health?

NOTES

CHAPTER 8
Spirit

The Spirit pillar in the good life definition encompasses faith, religion, spirituality, connection that goes beyond your own self—awe, expression, values, ethics and consciousness.

This is intentionally a very broad definition of Spirit. Some of you reading this may have either very strong beliefs or none at all, and thus be ready to skip this section altogether. For that reason I'd like to focus on spiritual practices and outcomes rather than specific beliefs.

An essential feature of many spiritual practices that I've experienced or been exposed to around the world is a state of grounded-ness and connection beyond yourself, which has the effect of suppressing or bypassing the ego, leading to a feeling of openness and an experience of love. Even practices such as meditation that involve intense self-focus on your own breathing simply use this as a device for you to escape your thinking mind and ego and to experience selflessness.

There are many benefits of this open and loving feeling. For one, it enables us to maintain perspective and see the bigger picture, not be dragged into "sweating the small stuff". It helps us to maintain a healthy level of consciousness that can be the source of peace and calm, yet also enables creativity and honest expression.

The quest I've been on for the past three years, to answer the question, *What is a good life (and how do we live it)?* and to develop a repeatable approach that allows professionals to live a good life, turned out to be a spiritual journey as much as an act of thinking and then putting words on a page. The reason it became a spiritual journey is that it caused me to look at, connect to, and act in the world in a different way.

It's impossible to face difficult life events and have to deal with these without reflecting on how we're living our life overall.

Completing a difficult challenge of any kind lets you understand who you are and what you stand for, and what is really important. You must know these things in order to find the strength to carry on and complete the challenge rather than give up.

Values and ethics may not seem important in good times, yet in difficult times they can be all that you have left to hold on to. As a bar-hopping 28-year-old in Hong Kong, unmarried, with a few dollars in my pocket and the world at my feet, values and ethics never gave me much cause for concern. But when it came to sitting in the intensive care unit at 1:00 a.m. with my four-week old daughter in Dallas, while dealing with the realities of my Dad's cancer thousands of miles away in Sydney, well, I was glad that I'd worked out what I was about and what I stood for. Doing so can give you a resilience and toughness that enable you to get through such seasons in life, rather than letting your world fall apart like an existential house of cards.

Your own good life journey may simply be a slight fine-tuning of your life philosophy and practices in order to get better results from them; if so, don't waste the opportunity to know and love yourself, and to live your values. There will come a time in your life when you or others will need the strength.

Exercise and creativity, done in the right way, can be spiritual practices too. For example, I find that riding my bike at White Rock Lake in the morning is part of my meditation on life. Pushing yourself physically can be an expression of personal honesty, and thereby a spiritual practice, since it challenges you to understand your limits as a human. It's impossible for me to kid myself that I can ride 20 laps when physically I can currently ride only five, yet the effort in trying to go farther involves a certain honestly—an abandonment of airs and graces.

Likewise, I've discovered that finding an avenue to express oneself in some creative activity is a spiritual practice, particularly if you feel that you can pour yourself into the activity without censoring yourself or holding anything back.

Each of the Five Pillars, in addition to being a focus area for planning how to use your energy and time, can be an avenue for spiritual development. By immersing ourselves in a pillar we learn about ourselves, and how we fit into the world.

Exercise 8.1—Vision for Spirit

Write a short paragraph that captures your vision for the Spirit pillar. What will your future spiritual state, sense of grounded-ness and moral anchor look and feel like? What practices will be a regular part of your life for managing your Spiritual state? How does a healthy spiritual state contribute to your overall life in the future?

Exercise 8.2–What Does Good Look Like?

Step 1—Identify key characteristics that drive your score.

Recall the score from 1-5 that you gave the Spirit pillar in Chapter 4. What are the key characteristics such as: grounded-ness, connection to others, peace and calm, belief or non-belief and level of engagement with others that led you to assign that score?

Step 2—Understanding sensitivity.

Determine how these characteristics would change if your score moved one mark up or down from where you are now. Also, identify what are the most important characteristics of the Spirit pillar for you.

Have you identified any non-negotiables?

Step 3—Descriptions for good.

In this step you'll write a description for each score from 1 out of 5 to 5 out of 5 for the Spirit pillar.

For example, my definition for Spirit 3 out of 5 is: remaining humble and grounded by seeking wisdom, tackling difficult challenges, experiencing awe and finding connection.

The key characteristics that would have to change to move my score to 4 out of 5 are: to demonstrate selfless love for others and to help those who have lost hope to experience hope. Achieving 5 out of 5 would entail extending my level of spiritual contribution to my community and beyond.

My score for Spirituality would be reduced if I no longer found the time to hear wisdom in others, or find connection on at least a weekly basis.

For each level from 1-5 write a short sentence or paragraph that describes that level and any key measures that apply.

Step 4—Add external role model practices and measures.

What practices and measures are others using to improve their scores for Spirit?

Exercise 8.3–Actions for Spirit Pillar

Make your list of actions now relating to Spirit. What can you do this week to build spirit in your community?

NOTES

CHAPTER 9
Expression

The Expression pillar contains the remaining activities that we engage in, operating in the mode of consumer or creator of an experience. The idea of the Expression pillar is to get you thinking about the degree of growth and expression existing in the activities you do and how these activities create your experience of life in the present and the future. The word expression comes from the Latin *exprimere* meaning to press out, so the Expression pillar also deals with how what you do impacts your community and society.

The lowest level mode of expression is consumption, where you experience both low growth and low expression. Examples of consumption activities include mindlessly sitting in front of the TV or surfing the Internet. You are passive in this activity, just letting it wash over you.

To upgrade this activity you could instead consume something that helps you to develop and grow, e.g., reading a book, or using your TV or Internet time to further an interest or personal project. This is still a low expression activity, but can lead to growth.

You could also upgrade the activity by increasing the amount of expression in what you're doing, though not necessarily the growth. Examples of high expression, low growth activities are ones such as casually playing a sport or a musical instrument.

A peak type of activity is one that is both high expression and high growth. An example could be jamming with a group of musicians, or participating in an ideas jam session with businesspeople. You can seek to perform a peak activity over time by undertaking a difficult challenge, such as running a marathon or writing a book.

An Australian executive that I spoke to summed this up by saying that each year he tried to do something that "scares" him. His meaning in life is derived from setting difficult physical challenges outside the work arena, which in turn lets him focus at work.

The simple message here is that it can be easy to fall into the trap of majoring in low-grade experiences that don't make you feel particularly good now, and don't help you later on. This is often the definition of what a comfort zone becomes, i.e., not really that comfortable. To have a better experience of life we should find or allow ourselves to be drawn into activities that allow us to express ourselves, or to grow, or both.

After a difficult period at work I allowed myself be drawn further into photography, cycling, and scuba diving. All of these activities let me express myself and to grow in different ways. I know myself well enough now to realize that I'm an expressive person (even though an introvert) and that although there were elements of my consulting career that let me express myself, I checked a lot of myself at the door before getting to work.

Instead of expression, some of you may think about this in terms of authenticity. Are you bringing the whole of yourself and the whole of your values to work, or to life for that matter, or are you holding back? Who are you?

Sometimes we underestimate the importance of pursuing our hobbies and interests since we don't comprehend their full benefits in maintaining mental and emotional health.

The final group of activities I want to talk about here are those in which we express ourselves, grow, *and* help others. A reliable way to upgrade your overall experience of life is to find energy and time for contribution activities (Chapter 15).

Exercise 9.1–Vision for Expression

Write a short paragraph that captures your vision for the Expression pillar. Which activities will be part of you and your future, allowing you to express yourself and to grow?

Exercise 9.2–What Does Good Look Like?

Step 1—Identify key characteristics that drive your score.

Recall the score from 1-5 that you gave the Expression pillar in Chapter 4. What are the key characteristics such as satisfaction, engagement, growth, expression, connection to others and so on that led you to assign that score?

Step 2—Understanding sensitivity.

Determine how these characteristics would change if your score moved one mark up or down from where you are now, and identify what are the most important characteristics of the Expression pillar for you.

Have you identified any non-negotiables?

Step 3—Descriptions for good.

In this step you'll write a description for each score from 1 out of 5 to 5 out of 5 for the Expression pillar.

For example, my definition for Expression 3 out of 5 is: moving from receive to transmit. Creating every day and every week rather than consuming. Having creativity and expression an obvious part of what I do and who I am.

To move my score to 4 out of 5: grow through playing a part in the growth experiences of others. To achieve 5 out of 5 would mean extending the contribution of my creativity and expression through the positive effects on others, and to a broader community.

My score for the Expression pillar would be reduced if I began to grow attached to and use consumption as my only means of self-expression.

For each level from 1-5 write a short sentence or paragraph that describes that level and any key measures that apply.

Step 4—Add external role model practices and measures.

What practices and measures are others using to improve their scores for Expression?

> For example:
> did you know
> that you can write a poem
> on your phone
> about whatever's on your mind
> while you're taking a ride
> or simply waiting in line?

Exercise 9.3—Actions For Expression Pillar

What can you do today to create something?

What part of your "dead" time that you spend in consumption activities could be upgraded to a hobby or interest that allows you to express yourself or to grow, or both? How could you express yourself and/or grow through helping others?

Make your list of actions now relating to Expression.

NOTES

CHAPTER 10
Summary and Quick Wins

The focus of Part One was on starting your good life journey, which included understanding what good looks like, knowing who you are and where you want to go, understanding where you are right now, and what needs to change in each of the areas represented by the Five Pillars.

All of these steps form part of a good life discipline called Directing Energy. Your personal energy emanates from your core values, character traits and passions, and is directed by the techniques of establishing a vision and creating a definition of good that encompasses all the important dimensions of your life.

The best way to a good life from this point on is to start implementing your vision and definitions of good by acting and interacting with others. There may be simple actions you can take (quick wins) which, although they may be small changes, will make a noticeable difference in your life. A quick win could simply be discussing with others elements of what you've done and what you've found by completing Part One of this book.

Don't lose the momentum from what you've already achieved; find one or more concrete actions that you can take. If what you'll do next involves a significant change and will take more than three months to accomplish, then you may want to dip into Part Three, which provides an example of how to approach such projects. Otherwise, put the book down and get started now. You can take a small action first and then read Part Two afterwards, rather than the other way around.

Many of you will reach this point with more to do in terms of completing the exercises or letting what you've done sink in before going any further. This is normal. If you are struggling to identify what to do next after completing the exercises, then let me suggest that you invest some further time in understanding what your three circles could really mean in practical terms.

Spend no more than one hour per circle researching the field or activity that the circle represents. Get some feedback from others. Identify one action that you can take that would allow you to experience each circle. Just do it! Even a small action (whether successful or not) will provide insight into the true nature of what you're trying to do that you couldn't get by spending the same time thinking or wishing.

Exercise 10.1—Part One Summary

Step 1 (Chapter 1)—The languages from Attainment to Being.

There are five languages that we use or can use to describe and set what we're focusing on now, and what we seek from life in the future. These are the languages that we use to create our vision, our goals, and even how we introduce and see ourselves.

The languages are:

- Attainment, i.e., what I have (job, house, possessions)

- Gratification, i.e., what I feel (pleasures, access to experiences)
- Importance, i.e., what I need (health, quality relationships)
- Meaning, i.e., what I stand for (beliefs and purpose)
- Being, i.e., what I am (living your values in everything you do)

Now that you've completed Part One, which language(s) will you aim to use to guide your life going forward? Why did you select those languages?

Step 2 (Chapters 2–4)—Self-insights, future direction, and where you are now.

What were the most important things that you learned about yourself, or reminded yourself about in the self-insight exercises in Chapter 2?

What role have core values played in the high and low points in your life?

What is the one thing that most excites you about the vision for the future that you've created?

Step 3 (Chapters 5–9)—Five Pillars.

You performed detailed exercises to define a vision, create a definition of good and identify actions for the pillars of Vocation, People, Health, Spirit, and Expression.

In your life today, how do you prioritize the pillars from most important to least important? Rank the pillars now, with 1 being most important and 5 least important. Do this ranking as if you were an impartial, third party observer of your own life, i.e., based on how you actually act and allocate your time and energy in practice (not as you wish that you did).

Next, rank the pillars in terms of how you want your life to operate, with 1 being most important and 5 being least important.

What has been the biggest insight in using the Five Pillars to analyze your life?

What is the most important thing that you need to do right now in order to allow your pillars to support each another in a better way?

Step 4—Structures of your life.

Which structures of your life such as routines, habits or organizations of work and relationships contribute to directing your energy in a positive way, and which detract from directing your energy in a positive way towards your vision?

How must these structures be reconfigured or changed in order for you to reach a good life?

Step 5—Your future personal story: Good Life Journey

Write a second version of your one-minute introduction that includes elements from everything you've covered so far in Part One. Incorporate elements of who you are, where you are now and where you want to go.

Read that introduction to yourself now and compare it to the first version you did in Chapter 4. How do you feel after reading the first and then the second version of your introduction?

Much to my wife's chagrin, I often like to wear T-shirts with the things I like to do on them: music, cycling, photography, diving, etc. This is no doubt a crime against fashion, but fairly regularly someone will come up to me in the street or at a store to talk about that topic. I share this somewhat comical story in order to make a serious point. How will the way you walk, talk, and look at the world attract your passions into your life, and allow you to transmit that passion to others?

Step 6—Next steps.

Identify three actions that you can take now, without having to complete the rest of this book.

Identify one reason why you're better able to live a good life now than before you completed Part One.

Now that you've started your journey, Part Two will help you to stay on track.

NOTES

PART TWO

STAYING ON TRACK

PART TWO—STAYING ON TRACK

In personal change, there is a stage between starting your journey and getting where you want to go in which invisible forces—such as fear, inertia, and a too-rigid attachment to our professional identity—can derail even the most important and needed change efforts. Part Two explores these forces—and proposes ways to overcome them.

The supporting disciplines for Part Two, grouped under the heading of "Unlocking Potential", are Perspective, Connection, Courage, Humor, and Contribution.

I described earlier how, around the time that my "good life journey" began, a series of major life events—achieving "success", getting married, moving countries, and starting a family—caused an existential crisis of sorts. As the "work me" and the "real me" continued to diverge, I reflected more and more on the larger purpose of my time on the planet.

Although I had a vision of a different life, I couldn't yet see a path to that vision, or connect with it emotionally and spiritually. An old but ever-present dream percolated within me, to start a business that would create positive experiences allowing people to have fun, meet others, learn and grow, but I hadn't acted on it. Having a vision that I wasn't pursuing felt like a constant reminder of just how off course my life was.

Perhaps, after completing Part One, you are asking yourself whether your vision is just a fantasy, or something you will actually make happen. For me, about six months after moving to the US, the walls of my life began closing in and I seemed to have lost the ability to see my future. Yet I could sense a small fire burning in the infinite blackness. A small fire within me.

This fire was a combination of tenacity and hope, a spark of potential that illuminated possibility. We are always but one spark away from lighting a path to a good life.

Then one night I found myself staring out across the icy waters of the Hudson from a hotel room in New Jersey. New York City lay before me—a place where people went to realize their dreams. The scene provided a powerful metaphor for my journey in life. I'd identified a vision (symbolized by the lights of Manhattan), which was a beacon for where I wanted to go. This vision seemed so near and yet so far, across water so cold that it had literal chunks of ice floating in it. I sat in a hotel that was warm and had its share of other creature comforts. But the hotel wasn't where I wanted to spend the rest of my life.

As I continued to gaze at the water, I began to see it less as a chasm and more as a medium of connection, an expression of potential. The water was a connector that would allow me to get to New York City or to anywhere else in the world for that matter. Challenges shouldn't stop us from living life. If anything, they should push us to start living life.

At the time when I was deeply thinking about "what next," I didn't lack potential or direction. But what I couldn't yet connect to was a sense of possibility—the will to persevere and then *create* a path. Rather than give up, I needed to find a pushing-off point that would allow me to traverse the river.

Realize that there exists infinite potential in the world and in you, even if you can't see a path to it right now. Find hope in that.

Life continued, and I battled the challenges that were being thrown at me. It felt as if I were wading through quicksand. I became a detective of my own life, seeking insight from challenges, as I took one step forward and two steps back. I looked for ways to recover more quickly from the steps back, and to find the means to prevent them.

I looked for bedrock in my search for a good life, and found through life's lessons what I've come to call the timeless human qualities of love, hope, and compassion. These are the source, the means, and the expression of our potential. They are forms of energy.

Understand that potential in practical terms is a process, not a thing. It is the process of knowing possibilities and following a path by finding perspective, connection, and courage while maintaining a sense of humor.

Some of you will have your own version of an unpursued dream, a path not taken. Perhaps you tried something and it didn't work. Perhaps you stopped dreaming. You need to believe again.

As I took my first tentative steps and missteps, unsure of the outcome, I began to see the world from a different angle, to connect with people differently and to find the will to commit to walking the path ahead of me.

Although potential and possibility can light a path, you still need to take the first step. This "closes the circuit" on your potential, making it real. As soon as you take the step, you'll be in a different reality. A new plane of possibilities will open up that you can't even see right now.

You'll realize that your potential is electric, or rather electrical. The path was in your own mind all along, in the potential energy of your own thoughts, intentions and beliefs.

You may find that due to its subject matter and the steps necessary to get there, the pursuit of a good life is by its nature a spiritual journey. It was for me, and continues to be. In Part Two, I try to condense this journey into a set of lessons learned about how to look both at life and our potential. I believe that each chapter, presented here as a thumbnail sketch, should be a starting point to further research and reflection on your part. As I compiled these insights, they began to form into what turned out to be the interrelated themes of perspective, connection, courage, humor and contribution. Sometimes the best lessons are not the ones that teach us something new, but those that remind us of what is truly important.

As professionals and leaders, we have significant skills, experience, and resources at our fingertips (what we know and who we know). This means that we have, on paper, a tremendous ability to make positive things happen in the world (i.e., what we could make happen). The biggest obstacles to reaching our potential and living a good life are therefore not external but internal, relating to our mindset (what we decide to make happen) and how we choose to relate to the world.

Our working lives and careers lead us to become blinkered and disconnected. We fail to find the courage and humor to know and follow possibilities that form a path to our potential. We become self-centered, forgetting that helping others is a reliable way to help ourselves live a good life.

Part Two comprises five chapters, each exploring a group of obstacles to a good life and laying out a path to overcome them. Chapter 11 covers perspective. Chapter 12 deals with nurturing deeper connection. Chapter 13 talks about finding courage. Chapter 14 describes the need to maintain a sense of humor. Chapter 15 makes the case for using contribution as a way to accelerate your journey to a good life.

If you are stuck in your personal change journey, then ask yourself, "Where am I lacking perspective, connection, courage or humor in what I'm trying to do, or the way I'm trying to do it?" and "How can I make a bigger contribution"? You may find yourself returning to Part Two as you are faced with key decisions, experiences, experiments and projects, which are the subject of Part Three.

CHAPTER 11
Focusing on the Right Things in the Right Way

Often we can get off track on our journey to a good life because our perspective is constrained—we fail to see possibilities, make informed choices, or envisage a future beyond the success we have already achieved in life.

This chapter describes three techniques that can allow you to stay on track:

- Focus on what is important
- Make your choices strategic
- Avoid the success trap

1. Focus on what is important

One of the keys to reaching your potential is learning to see again. We often have our eyes open, but not our minds. This is generally due to habits, beliefs, and other fixed ways of looking at the world, such as through the lens of our work, or through our overuse of the languages of attainment and gratification.

There are three elements in the art of seeing: focus, viewpoint, and openness.

FOCUS

Focus is the ability to direct your attention in a productive way. It is no accident that the spiritual practices of major religions include an emphasis on the importance of regularly focusing the mind in prayer or meditation. In our information-overloaded world, where our focus is bounced around constantly and our attention fragmented, the ability to focus, and to focus on the right things, can be the difference between living a good life or not.

The Three Circles, Five Pillars, your personal vision and the question of "What does good look like?" are all tools for building and maintaining focus on what is important to you. To live a good life, become aware of where your focus is at any time, and build habits and regular times to use the principles and practices in *The Good Life Book* (or whatever else you decide is important enough to focus on regularly). For example, I use the time first thing in the morning to do an inventory of my Five Pillars and the activities I was working on across all parts of my life. Before I began to make this a daily habit, weeks or even months would go by between my attempts to realign my focus with what was really important.

VIEWPOINT

We can focus so regularly on something that instead of our focus being like a microscope, it becomes like a permanent pair of glasses—a viewpoint or paradigm through which we view the whole world all the time.

Sometimes we get derailed from our good life journey because we're locked into a limited way of looking at the world, one that prevents us from seeing new possibilities and a path to reach our potential.

Viewpoint is most often the product of a comprehensive set of core beliefs built up over time. Or, for example, it could be the comfort and familiarity of using one of the "five languages" more than the others.

You can explore different viewpoints via a process of "standing in a different place." The simplest expression of this idea is that from one viewpoint you might see the glass of your life as half full; from another, half empty.

Below is a list of "places" that we could stand in to look at the world, and that I think have particular relevance to the question of a good life. At the start of my quest, I looked at the world from the point of view of the first word in each pair, but over time I found benefit in standing in the place represented by the second word.

The pairs of viewpoints are:

- Self or Others
- Fear or Promise
- Job or Portfolio
- Man or Nature
- Chaos or Order
- Industrial or Organic
- Scarcity or Abundance
- Born or Made
- Have or Be
- Thing or Process

Let me take the example of Born or Made. Do you believe that successful and happy people are born that way, or that they become so through their actions and attitudes? I often find that professionals who have achieved formidable success in their own right still believe that happiness is something that you're either born with or not.

A more productive belief is that happy people are made, and happiness is a process and a set of perspectives and attitudes, rather than an inborn character trait. This belief prompts us to take personal responsibility for our own happiness.

If you're getting stuck in a particular area of life, take the time to list the core beliefs or assumptions you have in that area. Next, perform a mind experiment in which you take the opposite idea or view. For example, you may believe that you're not naturally a healthy person. Now switch that belief around—choose to think that you are a healthy person and that you'll make time for health. How would you act, what would you prioritize, what criteria would you use to make decisions if you thought of yourself in this way? Making decisions from the point of view of a healthy person eventually helps to make your imagined state of health a self-fulfilling prophecy.

Another way to think about trying out different perspectives is in terms of moving from *if-then thinking* to *acting as-if.*

Many of us effectively live in the future, believing that an event, person or thing will make us happier, more balanced, "better." This is if-then thinking. If-then thinking makes you unhappy now, since you've made your happiness conditional on something you don't have. And it sets you up for failure, since *things* don't often bring us lasting happiness, while people only sometimes do—we must love ourselves first. So it's important to find opportunities to act as if you've already achieved the future state that you desire.

Next, you'll do a quick exercise on viewpoints related to an area that you are "stuck" in. If you can't identify such an area, then use one of the statement pairs in the list above, e.g., "Scarcity or Abundance."

Exercise 11.1—Viewpoint

Step 1—Find a current viewpoint.

Identify one area in life where you are stuck.

Step 2 — Document your beliefs.

Write five bullet points that would complete the sentence:

Area I am stuck… is . . .

For example:

Money is . . . the main thing I need more of to have a better life.

Select the statement that you feel most strongly about on the list.

Step 3—Take the opposite point of view.

Now perform a mind experiment in which you take the opposite view to your most strongly held statement/belief on the list.

For example:

Money is . . . not the main thing I need more of to have a better life.

Step 4—Write down what you see.

From this new point of view, how differently do you see the area that you are stuck in? What types of new approaches or solutions to your problem begin to emerge?

For example:

If money is not the main thing I need more of, then what do I need more of? Or, what combination of things? People, health, spirituality, meaningful work, the ability to express myself and grow. . . .

Using the scarcity example, you may have come up with an initial belief such as "It's a dog-eat-dog world." This is a fairly dark and—I've found—inaccurate view of humanity (though there are indeed individuals who operate this way). Taking the opposite view, "It's *not* a dog-eat-dog world" (i.e., there is abundance and enough to go around) moves the focus from what others *have* to what you will *do*, including how you'll work positively with others for mutual benefit.

A new perspective, even an imagined one, can open up a new plane of possibilities. The "rules" and "truths" of life are often reformulated in our minds as a result of a simple action and the change of viewpoint that comes with it. And often, in a way, that is positive for us.

OPENNESS

In addition to our conscious thinking, we see the world through our feelings, our emotions, our soul, and even our "gut." The logical bent of some professions can close us off to this way of thinking, dulling the power of our natural instinct and intuition. Given that life has rational, emotional, and spiritual elements, this can be like trying to eat a meal by listening to how it sounds. That is not a complete experience of the true nature of the thing! We need to open ourselves up in order to fully *see*.

Avenues I've used to become more open are as simple as spending time in nature (walking or cycling), expressing myself creatively, or asking others about their lives and then listening to what they have to say. I've also stopped the habit of mindlessly staring at my smartphone during every spare second. All of these experiences help to fine-tune my intuition and leave me open to see the world in the broadest and most objective way.

2. Make your choices strategic

Adopting a strategic perspective can be another productive way to look at the world. We're often told to be more "strategic." But what does that really mean? The word has become so widespread that I've recently listened to or read articles by earnest people on topics from "strategic gardening" to "strategic sleep." If everything has become strategic, then by definition nothing is. As a consultant in strategy and operations I looked for lessons on how to be more strategic in the things I was doing in life.

So, what is strategic thinking, why is it relevant to our work and life and how do we apply it?

Strategy is about making *choices* based on *insights* and assumptions concerning the external environment, and using internal capabilities to create *value*.

Let's look at each of the key elements of strategy and see how these apply to a good life.

CHOICES

For me the most important element of that definition of strategy is *choices*.

A choice sets direction, often involves significant unknowns, and provides context for further and more detailed *decisions* around the options that emerge. You may make a choice to try a new restaurant; a related decision would be what to select from the menu. A choice often limits the permutations of what decisions become possible. Certain types of choices we make on a regular basis (such as in the restaurant example); others may be blanket choices that stay in place until we change them.

An example of the latter is the choice we make in college about what career direction to take. This choice is often made with only rudimentary knowledge of what that career entails in practice, yet we often treat it as if it is a final decision, rather than recognizing that it remains a choice which we reaffirm every day when we get up to go to work.

To be more strategic, you can begin by identifying the key choices that you have in place and their impact on your life. Aside from our career choices, we make choices about, for example, what part of the country or world to live in, the person we choose to be our partner, and what our priorities are. Our life is a portfolio of choices. If you're able to follow the chain of cause-and-effect relationships in your life clearly enough, you'll find that behind everything that is currently good or bad there is usually, however far back, a choice.

Are your choices delivering the outcomes you expected? If not, then is the choice the problem? If so, then empower yourself to make a different choice.

If the choice is the right one, then not getting the outcomes you seek might relate to specific decisions you've made. Often we don't establish "whole life" criteria (such as prioritizing your Five Pillars) that establish a consistent basis for making decisions. As a result, you might find on analysis that decisions in one part of life are working against decisions or goals in another.

There is power in recognizing our choices—either to find the courage to change them, or to seek alternative variations of the same choice, (e.g., a different job in the same industry) or even to remind ourselves that we have indeed made a choice, and that we need to find out how to make the best of it.

During my personal journey it became clear that my choice of work needed re-examining. Working in a busy management consulting job also meant accepting a lifestyle—a sometimes exciting and always varied lifestyle, but also one that was mentally all-encompassing, and without an off-switch or a "slow" speed setting.

It became hard to even imagine doing something different. To be more strategic, I needed to change up the "bets" (i.e., choices, to use a gaming analogy) that I had on the table, finding a type of work that would allow me to open up my thinking and explore other ideas.

Exercise 11.2–Choices

What are the three most significant choices you've made that are affecting your life right now?

How is each choice performing? How is that choice affecting each pillar in your life?

If a choice is not performing well, is the problem the choice itself? If so, what are the alternatives? If not, is the problem with specific decisions or with the execution of your choices?

INTERNAL AND EXTERNAL INSIGHTS AND ASSUMPTIONS.

The possibility of making a good choice and our comfort level with that choice are both increased through effective use of internal and external information.

For an organization, internal information might relate to knowledge of what the company does well and is valued in the marketplace. External information might include trends around population and industry that affect the organization's products or services, or its competitiveness.

For our purposes, internal information is of the type you have already compiled in Part One. It includes answers to questions such as: Who are you? What is your idea of "good" in life? What are you good at (i.e., your strengths and weaknesses)?

Knowing yourself is a key to developing a personal strategy for your life, rather than just going with the flow or trying to be everything to everyone.

Many of us can benefit from a more systematic use of external information to evaluate key choices. This external information could be as simple as understanding competitive trends that affect your industry or occupation, or broader trends such as globalization and the aging population in many developed countries (we are, generally, both living longer and having fewer babies).

A concrete example of how broader trends are relevant to professionals concerns how automation, the global workforce, and cognitive computing are affecting and may potentially disrupt a broad range of professional careers. How might your job look different in the future? Will it exist at all in its current form?

Before deciding to leave my job, I tried to take a strategic view of how my career and the overall consulting industry were likely to evolve. I could see potential disruption and a difficult few years ahead for the industry, with small firms (and also individuals) in different parts of the world better able to compete with the existing large consulting houses, and with those large firms also seeking more globalization and automation in how they perform their work. Whether this trend would turn out to be just part of an economic cycle or a permanent change in how the industry worked, my analysis indicated that it was as good a time as any to explore a different Vocational Portfolio.

VALUE

We perform physical and mental activities in exchange for a package of financial value (salary and benefits) and non-financial value (experience, satisfaction, meaning). Taking a strategic view means trying to optimize both the value you get out of an exchange and how well the value aligns with your personal values (what I sometimes call your personal value-values equation).

The value that we create can be of the commoditized type (lots of people can do it) or differentiated (few people can do it). A skill can be specialized (requiring years of study and experience) and still be commoditized if many people in the market, or in your organization, can do it and are available to the market.

The market for value works on a supply and demand basis. Commodity skills typically deliver less value to the possessor of those skills than differentiated skills do, if we assume the same level of demand for each. Understand what type of value you are getting from your skills. In order to increase that value do you need to change markets, or to change the package of skills that you are marketing?

Work out what makes you unique and what you're passionate about, and then seek out the different markets for that bundle of skills and products or services that you can produce. Work out which situation offers the best financial and non-financial returns for you. The way to do this is to use a Vocational Portfolio along with the experimentation techniques that you'll hear about in Part Three.

By choosing to move from a consulting career to one that includes publishing content and running a small business, I've moved to a much more differentiated market, with both much higher and much lower potential returns than consulting, yet also with more potential flexibility, satisfaction, and meaning. In addition to other aspects of my personal burning platform I believed (and luckily still do) that this change in my vocational portfolio was well worth exploring.

You should review your strategic view periodically, to check that your assumptions still hold given a changing external environment, the changes in the value you can currently "bring to the table," and what you want from your value-values equation.

3. Avoid the success trap

Paradoxically, seeing ourselves as successful can hold us back. Many of you reading this are already successful—but are you living a good life?

When a personal day of judgment comes, the only evaluation of potential that matters is whether we've lived in line with our values and the timeless human qualities of love, hope, and compassion. Our success can limit our potential.

This section explores three questions:

- What is potential?
- Why does success limit our ability to reach our potential?
- How can we begin to further realize our potential?

WHAT IS POTENTIAL?

At the start of our schooling, potential relates to discovering our innate abilities and character traits (who we are). About the middle of our schooling, potential begins to focus more on our ability to use those abilities and traits to achieve outcomes (what we can do). The end of school casts potential in terms of the types of further education or job opportunities that we may be able to pursue (where we can go).

The concept of potential always has elements of both *who you are* and *what you can make happen*, yet by the end of our schooling we tend to think of potential in terms of specific goals rather than abilities or traits, and rarely if ever in terms of our ability to see and execute choices or our emerging personal values. By the time we begin work, potential comes to be defined in terms of how far (or how high) we can go in an organization or field, and perhaps the type of lifestyle that goes along with it (what we have).

Throughout this time from birth to work our potential hasn't necessarily narrowed; only our perspective on potential has. We've allowed our potential to become equated with our success in a specific job. Many of the professionals I've spoken to have formidable tools such as education, networks and experience, yet struggle to see any real possibility of doing something different with their lives. Just as our definition of good becomes fixed on attainment and gratification, so does our perspective on our potential. To fix the former we often have to first address how we see potential.

Right now, you might feel like you've painted yourself into a corner, and that the only way forward is to take another step on a path that leads to a destination that you don't want to go to. The truth is that you still have significant potential, but you simply must go through a process to begin to see that potential again and the path forward from where you are, including which choices you will make. Potential is doing the right things in the right way, not trying so hard that you manage to do the wrong things somewhat effectively.

You should always explore your potential from the place of your values. Potential as "being the best you can be" is fine if you stick to your values and don't get side-tracked by others' views of what you could or should do.

From talking to so many professionals over the years I've come to understand that so many of us do what we can do, yet still dream of doing something else. The "work me" saw potential as an obstacle course of projects and skills and promotions and office politics that I needed to traverse in order to become a global executive. The real me wanted to run a business that helped people through positive experiences.

The work me and real me maintained an uneasy equilibrium, since I feared that if I tried to reach my dream and failed, then it would be lost forever. The work me would somehow become my whole life rather than a choice. The pressure of trying to resolve work me and real me just after I got married preceded the flash of insight into my life purpose that I mentioned here earlier.

All of a sudden my potential wasn't to be found in a faraway land, but right there inside of me. Helping others who had lost hope was something that I could've started working on that very day.

That moment was a pure insight that the only potential that matters is one based on your values and the timeless qualities of love, hope, and compassion. Or, in other words, good expressed in the language of being. So why did it take years from that point to make a material change in how I spent my energy and time? The answer is identity.

WHY DOES SUCCESS LIMIT OUR ABILITY TO REACH OUR POTENTIAL?

There are three reasons why success limits our potential. They have to do with identity, characteristics of professional work, and what I call "comfort/good enough."

Identity, or self-concept, is a critical component of our potential. Success at anything usually comes as a result of focus and repeated effort (and perhaps some luck). Since work takes up so much of our time and mental energy, being successful at work can not only change how we think but also who we believe we are.

This may not seem like much of an issue, but what if you wanted to change your life in such a way that it no longer conformed to the norms of your profession? What if you lost your job? In these cases our job-biased self-concept can become like a set of blinkers, limiting the opportunities that we see. Loss of a job can mean not only that you are left without income, but also without self. The effect can be devastating.

I will now ask a simple yet essential question.

Exercise 11.3—Identity

To complete this exercise answer one simple (well, easily asked) question:

- Who am I?

Who are you? Answer the question now.

Without thinking, we describe who we are in terms of the job we have. From this place it can be difficult to see or to seriously entertain doing something different with your life, either inside or even outside of work. You can treat your job like it is a force of nature, like gravity, or somehow part of your DNA, rather than being a choice.

After quitting my job and running some pilot ideas for a small business, I can conclusively say that there is absolutely no external reason why I couldn't have done it 20 years earlier. Money or time or experience weren't limiting factors. I had even run a small business prior to joining consulting. The biggest limiting factor was fear of failure and the threat to my personal identity, which had become inextricably linked to my job as a management consultant.

For much of that 20-year period, whether I was "good enough" in terms of my ambition was based on whether I was travelling internationally, whether I was doing well at work and the extent to which I could justify that my work-hard, play-hard lifestyle constituted a good life. Fear and the rigidity of my professional identity prevented me from pursuing a dream as the target of my ambition.

As quitting my job became a real possibility, I was surprised that I felt a sudden remorse holding me back from making the call. This remorse was in fact a combination of fear of the unknown and pride. I'd spent almost two decades invested in a career, and the pain of "throwing that away" was acute. I took a deep breath and reminded myself of the concept of "sunk costs" as it applies to life.

What matters is not how much you've invested in the past, but the potential returns in future. Don't throw good money (or energy) after bad. Some of you reading this already know that you should be doing something different, and perhaps even know what that thing is, but you don't do it, because it is not yet how you see yourself. Or perhaps you are attached by pride to a job title, or fear that some person or people may judge you as a failure for wanting to change.

Exercise 11.4—Work Me and Real Me

Step 1—Identity keywords.

Select five words that best describe who you are and who you want to be. You can use the personal story exercise you did in Chapter 4 as an input for this step. Is your identity where you're from, your job, which sporting team you follow, what you're good at, where you live, your dreams, or that you haven't yet pursued your dreams?

Write down your five identity words now.

Step 2—Current state.

Do these keywords represent your internal identity or the identity you project to the rest of the world?

Which of these words do you feel uncomfortable with?

Which external obstacles (e.g., job, schedule) are preventing you from living your "real me" self?

Which internal obstacles (e.g., habits, self-beliefs) are preventing you from living your "real me" self?

Step 3—Evidence.

Taking an action that is uncommon for you can often provide evidence that you can use to prove to yourself that a future change of direction is possible.

Identify one thing that you can do to bridge the gap between how you define yourself now, and who you want to be in future.

There are several characteristics of professional careers that can themselves derail an effort to change.

The inherent bias towards consistency and being risk-averse in professional work can limit the possibilities we see. We also stop having time and the opportunity to have access to a variety of diverse experiences, people, and other ideas and inputs. This can easily translate into not taking chances in our careers and lives, even if the situation that we're in is not particularly great.

In any professional group there is a tendency toward group norms that perpetuate the status quo. It can be difficult to change your life if the only people you interact with are those who think and act the way you do. The strength of self-reliance in professional careers can turn into the flipside of loneliness, isolation, and poorer decision-making as a result of not consulting with others.

Even the strength that comes with specialization of knowledge in professional careers can limit our willingness to become generalists and beginners in exploring new possibilities in life. Many professionals struggle to see how they can make the world a better place, since they are looking at the world through their job description, not in terms of the full scope of their ability and responsibility.

On day one of our careers we didn't possess the skills and knowledge that we now have. Living a balanced life often means becoming a novice again, taking a chance, and recognizing that we have a lot to learn in order to master each pillar.

What held me back from trying to "help others that have lost all hope" more directly was looking for the perfect way to begin rather than just taking a small action and then working out what would come next from there. Of course there were also many occasions when the indirect route to a slightly better world, helping professionals and leaders who've lost hope of a better life, could have come unstuck too, given that I hadn't published a book before. It took years for me to believe that I could be the sort of person who'd quit their job to write a book. The only way to finish is to start.

One of the factors that attracts people into professional careers is the lifestyle and comforts that those careers often provide. Yet we can't comfort ourselves to a good life. Often, these comforts dull our senses to what is possible in life, and sap our energy to do something about it. The result can be that we use material comforts to try to compensate for the reality that our lives are not balanced or meaningful. When you worry how your frequent flyer or hotel reward status will be affected if you change your life, then that's reason enough to change. A pure focus on building a good lifestyle ahead of everything else can lead only to a *good-enough* life, not a good one.

For the majority of my career I was fortunate to have access to pleasurable travel and experiences, and for the most part never to have to worry about money. This type of gratification was enough to keep at bay a brewing existential crisis. And then one day it wasn't enough anymore.

HOW CAN WE BEGIN TO FURTHER REALIZE OUR POTENTIAL?

The work you've already done around self-awareness and the Five Pillars in Part One constitutes practical first steps to understanding the real you and what you truly need, as opposed to simply living the lifestyle that you've become accustomed to.

The next step is to begin to take actions—decisions, experiences, experiments, and personal projects—that allow you to engage with your future self (in whole or part) and to gather evidence supporting further actions.

In fact, even if the action you take is not a complete success, you'll at least understand better the nature of the thing you're trying to do. This increased understanding can be enough to get you to make a decision to further investigate the project, and not shut down the possibility that it represents.

Our identity doesn't change overnight. Instead, we move through incremental cycles of small change and reorientation. The process is almost like replacing a couple of pieces of a thousand-piece jigsaw puzzle every day with other pieces that make up a slightly different picture, and then looking at it from the other side of the room. The puzzle is still complete at the end of each day, but eventually (and after a period of "patchiness") we look at it and see that the picture has changed.

My identity evolved from being mostly about work to include photography and scuba diving and cycling as alternative parts of "who I am" in addition to my job as a consultant. Perhaps it was the increased level of expression associated with these activities that led me to an opportunity to teach a Consulting 101 course to new joiners at the firm. After that I taught business skills to social entrepreneurs through the firm's corporate social responsibility program. And after that I did a deeper dive by supporting a charity focused on helping social entrepreneurs grow. As a result of working more and more with people who have a different worldview, my own worldview changed.

Simple ways to explore your potential include making a point of interacting with people outside your normal circle, or reading a magazine on a topic that you've never read about before, in a coffee shop that you've never been in before. In the past, I've also made a practice of taking a slightly different route to work every day. These seem like small changes, but they train you to get used to thinking differently, and in a way that really counts when it comes time to decide whether to change your life. You form the belief that you are a person who is open to change.

❦ ❦ ❦

The chapter you've just read aims, in a roundabout way, to solve the seeming paradox of why professional people with so many resources at their disposal are often unhappy, and seem powerless to do anything about it.

We stop seeing. We make many decisions but few choices (including the choice to live a good life). We fail to see the powerful but often invisible barriers to change that come with our success and are part of the nature of professional work.

CHAPTER 12
Nurturing Connection

We can get off the track to living a happy, balanced, and meaningful life because we fail to connect with others, and with our potential.

This chapter describes three techniques for nurturing connection in order to stay on track:

- Mind your minds
- Escape the professional bubble
- Reclaim love

1. Mind Your Minds

The primary tool for much professional work is the brain, so advances in neuroscience and psychology that I read about during my quest were of great interest to me, as they are for many of the people I spoke with. Clearly, our thinking affects how we see the world and what we can achieve. Yet I also observed that by always using only one type of thinking, specifically logical thinking, we can become disconnected from the full experience of life, limiting our possibilities for living a good life. Reading more brain science articles wasn't the answer. Instead, I devised a model of minds (yes, mind*s*) based on my own experience.

I've found that it is most useful to conceptualize thinking as originating in five separate but interrelated minds, each with its own "personality," and also to use the metaphor of a "meeting of minds" to explore how each mind interacts with the others. Imagine a scene in which these minds are "people" participating in an unruly business meeting, with you as a neutral facilitator.

The five minds are:

- Universal Mind
- Primitive Mind
- Classic Mind
- Ego Mind
- Hidden Mind

Universal Mind

The Universal Mind or God Mind refers to, in my model, the world of ideas, possibilities, and energy that extends beyond our conscious minds and physical bodies.

It's easy to get wrapped up in our own thinking and forget that we are part of a much greater universe of ideas, energy, and possibility, even if that universe is not always visible to us.

I'm writing this paragraph sitting in an armchair at a local library surrounded by racks upon racks of books. The topics include art, design, war, geography, history, and biography. Clearly, these books are physical representations of knowledge beyond my thinking mind. Yet the books are also a codification of earlier electrical impulses in the brains of the authors who wrote them (whether living or dead), and before that the experiences and phenomena that inspired these authors. If I close my eyes, I can no longer see the books, but that doesn't mean that they no longer exist. To access this world of ideas I have to engage, to take a book off the shelf.

Using the metaphor of an unruly meeting-room of minds, the Universal mind is that person who chirps up with only a few words to say, cutting through the chatter and framing the whole discussion in a new light and pointing it in an unforeseen but productive direction.

You may have had the experience of plucking an idea "out of thin air." As I've begun to spend more time in highly expressive activities, I've also had the "thin air" experience more and more. Often, when doing creative writing, I feel like the words are somehow coming from the ether, through me and then onto the page.

Many of us, when we're stuck or stressed, tend to close down and cut ourselves off. If we believe that the world of possibilities exists outside of ourselves, then cutting off would be exactly the wrong thing to do. Instead, we should open ourselves up. We should open up our consciousness.

Consciousness is our ability to see the true nature of things, to gain perspective and see interconnections and new possibilities.

In my experience, consciousness moves through different levels, from low to high. Many of us have had the experience of high consciousness (fully open mind) in which we have a panoramic view of our lives — past, present and future. We can see our habits and look at the solutions to our problems in an unconstrained way.

Perhaps these moments happen on holiday or, at the other extreme, as the result of a life event or crisis which shakes us out of a mental comfort zone and forces us to see things as they truly are. We have low-consciousness moments too, where we're unable to even make simple decisions. We are frazzled, burned out—it's as if we're stumbling around in the dark.

First thing in the morning is when many of us experience a medium-high level of consciousness (at least, perhaps, after we've had a cup of tea or coffee). At that time I have a high level of clarity of thinking that allows me to look for patterns and interconnections in information (as part of my work) or to find solutions to seemingly intractable problems that require logic and focus. The night (especially in the days before I had kids) was a time when my mind would explore possibilities, and this was also a good time for creative writing.

To experience different levels of consciousness, track your energy levels and the times of the day at which you do your clearest thinking, are most creative, and are best at dealing with other people.

Primitive Mind

The Primitive Mind is the one most closely wired to our physical body and physiology. Since its purpose is to maintain our survival, it is largely driven by impulses. The Primitive Mind reacts when we get a fight-or-flight response to public speaking, or when we overeat out of stress. The Primitive Mind seeks pleasure and comfort and tries to avoid pain.

In the imaginary meeting room of minds the Primitive Mind is the one always looking at their watch and wondering when lunch will arrive, or blurting out a reactive response to whatever is happening at the time.

Since the minds are interconnected, the Primitive Mind responds using the limited tools at its disposal to deal with signals of pain coming from any of the other minds—sometimes in an inappropriate way. For example, if our ego is hurt and we have a bad day at work, then the Primitive Mind urges us to engage in retail therapy or a session at the pub.

The way to deal with the Primitive Mind is to be aware of impulse- or compulsion-driven behavior, then either intercept those impulses or prevent them from arising. I've found that having a plan in place (see Part One of this book) and developing practices to manage the issues on your mind so that there are as few "loose ends" lying around as possible are effective ways to prevent your Primitive Mind from being on guard all the time (which is stressful and tiring).

We can manage loose ends by having a personal system to manage to-do activities and having clear criteria for prioritizing them. To convert a to-do list from a source of bad stress to a source of good stress, make sure that you take a little extra time to identify the next concrete action for every item on your to-do list.

Classic Mind

The Classic Mind is the logical and conscious part of your brain. Although we believe that our logical minds are objective and "all-seeing" they are in fact subject to fixed ways of thinking and old beliefs that when examined often no longer make logical sense.

The Classic Mind is the person in our imaginary meeting who always plays things by the book and is like a computer, always rational. This person has the sometimes annoying habit of not wanting to make a decision in the meeting, instead wanting to gather more information and facts.

We may believe that it's possible to think our way to a good life. But although positive thinking can be useful on a short-term basis, helping us to take an action, it is rarely enough by itself to create sustainable change.

A good life is not a logical puzzle to be solved, nor a purely intellectual concept. We have to accept that as humans our path to a good life will also be an emotional and spiritual one, and therefore we must open ourselves up to emotional and spiritual ways of engaging with the world in order to live a good life.

Living a good life often involves taking a series of actions that are uncommon for you. Sometimes this is characterized as taking a "leap of faith," but you may feel more comfortable thinking in terms of making a small effort to try new things. By keeping things small you can limit the downside risk that any action will be bad in a life-changing sense. On the upside, if the action leads in a positive direction you can quickly take another step, emboldened by the new perspective you arrive at after taking the first.

Ego Mind

The Ego Mind is simply your sense of self and how you see your place and value in the world.

In our imaginary meeting the Ego Mind is the one reacting in a prideful way, or else sticking to their guns at all costs. In acting this way, the Ego Mind can appear at times proud, confident, stubborn, or even arrogant, depending on the circumstances.

I think that most of us have at one time or another directly experienced the truth of the saying that "pride cometh before a fall." Pride cuts us off from the world rather than connecting us, and blinds us to information and possibilities that could be helpful to us. Our ego compels us to speak when we really should listen and reflect.

While Ego can spur us on to tackle ambitious goals, it can also become a wall that cuts our thinking off from the world of ideas and possibilities (i.e., the Universal Mind). A simple technique when you're stuck in life is to ask, "How is my ego building a wall that it causing me to get stuck?" Perfectionism, and the related fear of failure, is perhaps the most insidious example of the ego-wall I just described. Our ego seeks to isolate itself from change, even though the change may be good for us.

I've begun to try to practice humility as much as possible (perhaps not the easiest thing to do for a management consultant) and to approach my journey to a good life based on an honest recognition of what needs to change and what needs to be done in practice, rather than living in a dream world where everything is perfect but nothing gets done.

Hidden Mind

The Hidden Mind is our subconscious and also the interface to the emotional and spiritual aspects of us that affect and are part of our thinking in a holistic sense.

Part of the magic of human change is that we can issue a task to our conscious mind and the solution comes from our subconscious as an insight, as if an invisible hand was guiding our actions.

As the final "person" in our metaphorical meeting room, the Hidden Mind is the one who asks questions which lead the group discussion forward, as opposed to offering solutions directly.

Like the hidden part of an iceberg, our Hidden Mind is the expanse that we don't see and is below the waterline, yet contains most of the mass. This mass becomes relevant when we try to change. Either the momentum of that mass is on our side and we can change, or it is against us and we fail to change. The vision you created in Part One is a tangible way to get your subconscious on board to help you reach a good life. To make that work you have to review and engage with your vision on a regular basis. You have to read and *need* your vision.

To get the most from the insights emerging from the hidden parts of our thinking, we have to make space in our lives and in our thoughts. I've felt considerably more balanced and refreshed by drastically cutting back on the time I spend on social media, with my smartphone or watching news in the morning.

The insidious effect of my cramming every increment of time and attention with stimulus was that it disrupted my mind's natural mechanism for dealing with stress and for processing the interface between the thinking, emotional and spiritual aspects of myself.

Cycling, going for walks, or even reading a book also provide time for this type of engagement with my Hidden Mind. It's no coincidence that when I felt stressed at work these were exactly the types of activities that I'd cut back on. Exactly the same activities that would've helped me regain perspective to deal with difficult times.

Exercise 12.1–Self-talk

To close out this section you'll do a simple exercise. Over the next day, be aware of your own thoughts and self-talk (the voice we hear inside our head) and try to answer the following questions:

Is the voice always the same in every situation, or are there different voices?

What point of view or priority does the voice have?

Do you believe that your self-talk is helping you to reach a good life, or the opposite?

2. The Professional Bubble and Humanity

As you bounce through life from meeting to meeting, phone pressed to ear and with eyes locked on email during every waking hour, do you ever get the sense that you are getting cut off from the rest of the world?

The consulting lifestyle made me feel like I was living in a bubble a lot of the time. Sometimes, I'd eat all three meals at the office. At other times, I'd visit multiple countries on a business trip and still not interact with more than a handful of people.

During the time I wasn't working I would play hard. Later, after getting married, I tried to eke out a few quality hours with my small family in the moments outside work (my extended family living interstate or overseas).

This type of routine didn't leave me much time to reflect on the breadth and wonder of humanity, and I had the feeling of being on autopilot.

While in London I stopped off daily at a local coffee shop midway through my ten-minute walk from home to my office along the Thames. The shop knew my order since I got the same thing every day. Typically I was lost in thought about work and a good life.

One day my order was taking longer than usual, and the cause was a group of tourists trying to work out the English currency, which is based on numerous small coins. I was frustrated that I was going to be late for a meeting, given my very finely-tuned departure time from home. When they'd finally paid and I'd gotten my order and left the coffee shop I had the following thought (no lie): *People are holding me up from working out what is important in life.*

This thought surprised me enough to break me out of my trance, and I chuckled to myself. *People are the most important thing in life,* I thought as I drank my coffee and walked. That the biggest thing I had to worry about was how quickly my coffee was delivered had to be a sure sign that I'd taken up residence in a bubble, and without even realizing it.

Becoming disconnected from the world around us can be an obstacle to living a good life. This can be the result of never being fully present, or not experiencing the timeless qualities that make us human, such as love, hope, and compassion.

Exercise 12.2—Escaping The Bubble

Step 1—A typical week.

Reflect on how you spend your time in a typical day or week. How often do you have occasion to interact with someone who holds different beliefs, or is from a different socio-economic background than yourself?

When was the last time you learned something new that wasn't to do with work?

How many hours in a typical week (both inside and outside of work) are unscheduled?

Step 2—Review your answers.

Based on how you spend a typical week, would you say you live in a bubble or not?

If you are living in a bubble, then how does it feel? What aspects of life do you believe you're missing out on?

Step 3—Action.

What is one simple action that you can put into place that will draw you out of your bubble (get you out of your comfort zone) at least once a week?

There is an even more insidious outcome from being cut off as a result of your professional career. That is to believe that your problems are cosmic and the solutions are personal rather than the other way around.

It's possible to believe that our problems, including the challenge of finding the meaning in life, somehow have cosmic significance. Thinking about our problems in this way can make us selfish and self-centered. We can search the earth for solutions to the problem of finding meaning or finding happiness, ignoring those solutions that are hidden in plain sight (for example, in the people that surround us). While working in New York, I observed how a cold winter's morning was one of the few situations that we all have to deal with at the same time. The snow and ice unite us in a small but honest expression of life.

Our individual problems, including the difficulty in finding meaning in life, are common to all humans. But the solutions to these common problems are cosmic, in that they often can be found beyond the places we can think ourselves to. We reach those solutions by keeping ourselves open emotionally and spiritually, and through interaction with others.

Exercise 12.3—Common Problems and Cosmic Solutions

Step 1—Identification of problems.

Identify one significant area of life where you are stuck.

Step 2—Get cosmic.

Identify three people in your network who can potentially help you with your pressing issue, and also three people that you can help.

Step 3—Make a request to others. Respond to a request for help.

Engage the three people in your pressing issue. Be on the lookout for an opportunity to help someone you know (or someone you don't).

❧   ❧   ❧

At the time of this writing, there are people in all countries of the world who are still suffering the aftereffects of the global financial crisis and the longer, continuing phenomenon of globalization. I don't believe that we can find the answer to our own happiness without doing something to improve that of others.

3. Reclaim Love

An essential part of nurturing connection is moving beyond intellectual thought to address your emotional and spiritual sides.

I've found that:

- Meaning, happiness and how you see balance are not purely intellectual things but are holistic, connecting the head, heart, and soul
- You must build your vision of a good life using a dose of naked honesty and self-awareness rather than building on the shifting sands of ego
- Personal transformation doesn't happen overnight. You'll need to be aware of, and be practiced at using, your emotional and spiritual sides to make course corrections and overcome obstacles and setbacks

Love as both an emotion and a form of connection is, in my view, widely misunderstood in its broader application to transforming the way that we look at and experience life. That is something I'll seek to address now.

A systematic way to increase the meaning and satisfaction in your life is to try to upgrade the degree to which you live and experience one or more of what I think of as the seven loves.

The seven loves covered in this chapter are:

- Self-love
- Romantic and sexual love
- Love of friends and family
- Selfless love in society
- Love of God/connection
- Awe and wonder
- Expression and immersion

Self-love

Self-love is knowing, liking, and accepting oneself based on an honest awareness and understanding of one's strengths and weaknesses, preferences, curiosities, and genuine aspirations (as opposed to aspirations based on attainment of status and possessions). Being comfortable in your own skin is part of healthy self-love.

Self-love is not vanity or self-delusion, which are both driven by pride and are therefore not honest. Endless critique and inward focus are also not self-love and can lead to a spiral of self-doubt and rumination. Being overly critical is not honest, since it ignores your personal strengths and unique opportunities.

Many veterans of self-help are stuck in a cycle of self-doubt which many supposedly "self-help" books seem to foster. We could arrive at the belief that we need to *buy* a change because of something we lack, rather than *be* a change based on the strengths we already have.

Clearly, self-love is a foundation of the journey to a good life, since it allows you to be aware of what needs to change, and to have the courage to go ahead and change it. Self-love gives you a defense against self-destructive behavior, which can easily occur if we're not happy and not honest with ourselves.

The transformational journey you go on as you move from other people's definitions of success to your own is an example of honesty. Instead of believing that you're a failure because you want or need to change, you could realize that this is a common situation in life. Realize also that the first steps to living in a different way are often more tentative and less perfect than we may expect or want.

Developing greater self-love happened for me through a process of moving from a singular definition of life—"work-hard, play-hard" (which can be a fairly brutal and unloving mode to be in)—to a more multi-dimensional view of myself based on my interests in photography, writing, cycling, and fitness. Later my self-love was increased through other types of love represented by charity work, getting married, and becoming a father.

Exercise 12.4—Self-love

Following on from the exercise that you completed in the first section of this chapter about self-talk, in this exercise you'll evaluate your level of self-love.

Over the next three days, assess the degree of self-love that you are applying in your thoughts, decisions, actions and interactions with others.

To do this, look out for situations in which an outcome is created that is either positive or negative for your life in the long run. For each type of situation reflect on what you believed about yourself at the time the situation was occurring.

For example, if you reach for a big piece of cake after a tough day, and yet you are struggling with maintaining your target weight, then is your self-talk saying that your situation is hopeless, so one piece of cake doesn't matter? When things have gone right for you, then what was your self-talk saying at that time?

Have fun with this exercise, and at the end of the three days remember to write up what you've discovered.

Romantic and Sexual Love

Healthy romantic and sexual love is interdependent with self-love. Sometimes knowing and loving yourself comes first, and allows you to have an interdependent and balanced relationship with someone else. People tend to be attracted to others who love life. In other times the love of another person can help to unlock or ignite your self-love, helping you to see something that you were previously blind to.

It's an unfortunate fact that professional life can be a blocker to both establishing and maintaining strong relationships. It can be difficult to meet others given the demands of work and (sometimes) the narrow set of individuals you come in contact with. The demands of work can also distract from the "people aspects" of your life outside of work. While I don't profess to offer any winning matchmaking advice, I can honestly say that I've applied good life thinking at every stage of life, from being a bachelor to being a married person with kids. Doing so in one way or another has always yielded something productive in my relationships with others.

As you progress through this book, please be aware of the need to bring others close to you on the journey, and maintain with them a shared vision of the future. For example, if your partner values security, then it's likely that if you talk in vague terms about big changes in your life, this will set off a series of negative triggers in him or her. Your partner's ego may also be challenged if there is a risk that these changes will affect social standing or lifestyle.

Love of Family and Friends

Our love of family and friends is a key ingredient in a rich and meaningful life. Family and friends support us, and we in turn support them through the ups and downs of life. Professional life can restrict the amount of quality time and energy we have to invest with family and friends. In the short term we may not notice how that is detracting from the balance and quality of our lives, though we may become more and more isolated over time.

Family and friends are people and stakeholders in themselves, too—they have their own objectives and preferences in terms of what they bring to and take from the relationship. Managing the needs of others is a complex yet necessary part of the process of personal change. Sometimes, friends and family have priorities that are not aligned with your own, and they may act in opposition to what you are trying to achieve.

It is interesting that one side effect of the proliferation of "friends" on social media is that we are faced with the challenge of how to allocate our energy and love to this wider group—risking distraction from the deeper, true relationships that support and enrich us.

You may decide that a more systematic approach to planning opportunities to engage with your friends is in order—spending more time with people who are supportive and give you energy, and less with those who constantly drain your energy. Often, we need new friends and acquaintances to enable us to reach our potential.

Selfless Love In Society

The concept of selfless love is sometimes called by the ancient Greek word *agape*, and is close to the idea of charity. (In Christianity the word *agape* is used exclusively when referring to God -love; see next section.)

Selfless love is not a new concept, though it can sometimes be hard to find evidence of it on the evening news. The concept of reconnecting with humanity, which was discussed in the last section, is in fact a form of selfless love.

It is difficult or impossible to feel this type of love if you are coming from a self-centered and selfish place, or if you're running around with your blinkers on, decrying the state of society but not doing anything to change things.

A simple way to begin sharing selfless love is to be aware of those who cross your path each day—are you making their lives better or worse? Are you showing them any selfless love or compassion? Can you help to increase the positive feeling in their day?

There is also the concept of "paying it forward." I think most of us can understand the concept of reciprocity, i.e., you do something for someone and then they do something for you. This is the basis of many business relationships. Paying it forward is different; instead of repaying the person who helped you, you decide to help someone else in the way most appropriate for that person. This is powerful, in that the effect of the good deed is multiplied. The more you do this, the easier it becomes to escape your own ego and live in an ongoing state of openness, where you see the good in society. Yes, it really works.

Love of God/Connection

For many people a connection with their God is their primary source of love, stability, and peace of mind. Traditional religious practice often involves ways to build and sustain this love through group prayer, charity, and community. There may also be an opportunity for you to connect more and further strengthen your faith through teaching and supporting others.

One of the key components of spirituality is awe and connecting to something greater than yourself—whether you label that God, the Earth, or the Universe, or something else.

For that reason I've added awe/wonder and expression/immersion to my list of types of love. Both of these are spiritual highways that can lead you to a greater level of connection.

Awe and Wonder

The type of wonder that I want to talk about briefly is that which you can experience in nature. The stars at night, a mountain range, the colorful vista of a coral reef — these things elicit a feeling of connection to something greater than you. If you think that including awe here stretches the definition of love, then think about the concept of reverence or respect that is inherent in awe.

The age and scale of nature dwarfs our individual selves—yet we too are part of nature. In our increasingly urban and connected world it can be easy to lose touch with nature, and thus lose touch with ourselves as well.

Creativity and Immersion

At the risk of being too abstract, the final form of love that I want to discuss is that relating to expression and immersion.

Expressing yourself honestly is a way to link head, heart, and soul. Expression is rarely a purely intellectual exercise or one that you can perform by closing yourself up. One of the quickest and most reliable ways to change your life—and I've both experienced and seen it again and again—is to find yourself a creative outlet. This is especially important if you don't see yourself as a "creative person" (whatever that means). You'll notice the most difference when you switch from "receiving" to "transmitting," to use a radio analogy.

Immersion is an example of how you can lose yourself in an experience or subject. This could be, for example, playing a sport, or music, or immersion in work activities. Mihály Csíkszentmihályi has probably the most popular and well-known expression of this idea in his book *Flow*. He describes a state in which you are so engrossed in an activity that you lose track of time. This "flow" state is associated with a more positive experience of life.

Immersion can also occur over a longer period—for example, when you inhabit the fictional world of a novel, or perhaps even reading this book. Often the deep mental involvement that is a key component of immersion can bypass the ego and logical elements of your mind. We can act more instinctively without the constraints that fear and the need to protect one's identity can place upon us, and thus feel more connected to the world around us.

Exercise 12.5–Bringing Love

To close out the chapter, select one type of love that you've just read about and identify one action you can take in the next week to apply it in your daily life. Of course, I'm not talking about making unwanted advances to unsuspecting people; just keep it simple. If you are feeling ambitious, then you could try to do one thing per day for a week!

CHAPTER 13
Finding Courage

We get off the track to a good life when we fail to find the courage to change. We allow short-term comforts to prevent us from seeking long-term peace of mind. We fail to exercise our liberties. We don't define happiness for ourselves.

The three techniques related to finding courage are:

- Stretch yourself
- Embrace freedom
- Build happiness

1. Stretch yourself

Most of us would say that peace of mind is an important part of the good life, but when we say "peace" each of us may mean something different.

What is peace of mind to you?

To my wife, peace of mind means security, while peace of mind for me is, for example, the knowledge that I'm doing something that puts me on track towards reaching my full potential.

Understanding what peace of mind meant to me and then pursuing it has *not* turned out to be a very peaceful process, at least if the definition of peace is stillness, comfort, and the absence of stress.

We all too often try to deal with problems in our lives by sinking back into our so-called comfort zone. Yet, over the long term, that comfort zone often isn't particularly comfortable. The experience that we feel in our comfort zone can be more like a low-grade yet long-term discomfort that we deem preferable to the seemingly higher intensity but short-term discomfort of making a change in our lives.

People stick with what's familiar—jobs, relationships, habits, just about anything—even if they know it's not right for them. Sooner or later in every journey to a good life, you will need to find the courage to change.

To explore the idea of courage a little more, let's look at the Serenity Prayer. There are two versions that I am aware of.

This is a version of the Serenity Prayer (attributed to Reinhold Niebuhr in in the 1930s) that I was not familiar with, but that I now prefer:

> *Father, give us courage to change what must be altered,*
> *serenity to accept what cannot be helped,*
> *and the insight to know the one from the other.*

There is another version that you may be more familiar with:

> *God grant me the serenity to accept the things I cannot change,*
> *courage to change the things I can, and the wisdom to know the difference.*

Let me ask you—what frame of mind would you be in if you repeated the first version to yourself in difficult times? What about the second one? Which do you like better?

There are two reasons why I like the first version better:

- It speaks about *us* rather than *I*. The message is that we all have common problems that we must face in life.
- The focus is on courage to change, rather than acceptance. It is too easy to seek false comfort in acceptance, as opposed to finding the courage to seek the right answer and then follow what you find.

Sometimes we stick with a belief that we find comfortable, even though it is false, since it prevents us from experiencing pain. A common example is "I'm too old," as in "I'm too old to change careers." These falsehoods are a type of convenient self-deception. We prefer to deceive ourselves rather than face up to the truth that we need to change. As a result, we push the pain into our subconscious, and the effect of that pain seeps out into our lives in unpredictable ways.

Exercise 13.1–Accept or Change

Step 1—Create a list of reasons/excuses.

Create a list of the common reasons (excuses) that you give yourself concerning why you can't make a change that would likely be positive in your life.

Step 2—Analyze your answers.

Examine each of the reasons on your list and answer the following question: Is this reason really valid/true?

What evidence can you find that supports this reason? What evidence can you find that supports the *opposite* of this reason?

What benefit are you getting for believing any reason that, on examination, is a falsehood? What is the benefit that you'd get by giving up this reason or excuse and then making a change in your life?

Step 3—Action.

Where you have identified a belief that is holding you back in life, identify one small action that you can take in the next week to disprove or invalidate that belief.

For example, if you believe you are too old to do something, can you find and then talk to someone who is the same age as you (or older) and has done what you aim to do? It is important that you also communicate with this person, not just know that they exist. It is a lot easier to ignore something that you've read on the Internet than it is to ignore somebody telling you—and embodying—how to make the change, and perhaps even offering to help.

Courage is like a muscle. It is something that we can develop through training—through something as simple as trying new things that stretch our comfort zone. By training ourselves in this way we prepare ourselves for bigger challenges, and are more likely to act with courage when those challenges arise.

Exercise 13.2–Expanding Your Comfort Zone

For the next month, try to do one thing per week that "scares" you.

Keep this simple. Identify a small action that you could take that you've thought about previously but not done, or that you've seen others do and are curious about.

There are folks who must face terrible circumstances every day in order to survive. We could look at their situation and conclude that we should be grateful for what we have (which we should), and as a result do nothing to try to improve our own lives. Yet a personal definition of courage is one that relies on connecting to and using strength from your heart. Even (perhaps especially) in a life filled with comfort and conveniences, we still need to find the courage to be true to ourselves and to overcome the inevitable obstacles to finding sustained happiness, balance, and meaning.

Sometimes helping others is a way to find the courage to change ourselves.

2. Embrace freedom

Liberty, including personal freedoms, is something that we take for granted, yet it was important enough to make it into the US Declaration of Independence as part of the "unalienable" rights to "Life, Liberty and the pursuit of Happiness".

Liberty is not something we achieve and then never lose. Instead, we must find courage and take personal responsibility for the exercise and defense of our liberties, as well as for extending them where it makes sense to do so.

Time and time again in my quest I've circled back to the societal aspects of a good life. How is our pursuit of a good life influenced, either positively or negatively, by institutions such as business and government, and by cultural norms? At best, I found a mixed picture—progress on some fronts but a slipping back on many others. Above all, I sensed that it is no time to be apathetic and to simply go with the flow, or to expect others to protect our liberties for us.

There are five liberties in particular that I believe warrant special mention in this chapter. They are:

- The freedom to define happiness and success for yourself
- The freedom of how and if to consume and create
- The freedom to define how and where to work
- The freedom to participate in community and government
- The freedom of knowledge and discourse

The Freedom to Define Happiness and Success For Yourself

A common definition of success is the middle class dream of "do well at school, get a good job, get married and then raise a family." This is but one definition of success in life, as is "self-actualization" or "the pursuit of intellectual and spiritual development," or simply "to be happy." The point here is that you have the responsibility to construct your own definition of success and happiness in life despite social pressure, real or perceived, to do one thing or another. The alternative is to try to make a definition that doesn't fit you work, or adopt one conjured up by a company trying to sell you something.

As I travel around the US and to other countries I detect a certain incredulity about why I'd even consider quitting a job that other people would "kill for" in order to pursue a simpler and happier life. Yet you can't live life based on what other people want or don't have, just as you can't live life based on what others do have.

The Freedom of How and If to Consume and Create

We live in an age of vast and sometimes paralyzing choices, given the number and variety of products and services we can have instant access to. Every whim, intention, or fear is monetized, with instant gratification just a click away. We have become petulant children with too many toys, not valuing or being grateful for what we have.

In preparation for quitting my job, I started cutting back on all non-essential expenditure. Whenever it came time to buy something, I'd try to put it off for a week or longer. Instead of a meal out, I'd cook at home. Instead of a nicer bottle of wine, I'd try to find a quality bottle at a bargain price. You can see that this is hardly ascetic, yet a strange thing happened. Buying less actually made me feel better, not worse. The things I'd been consuming had been consuming me—adding to my waistline or cluttering up my space. The freedom not to consume is one that is worth exercising from time to time.

It's probably not an overstatement to say that some people felt threatened when I talked about my more "minimalist" lifestyle. Part of exercising your liberty not to consume is to define people not by what they have, but by who they are.

When you do consume you have the right to demand quality and integrity from those businesses that you deal with. The businesses I respect the most are those that are interdependent with the communities that they operate in, rather than independent of them. Not all businesses operate this way, and each dollar you have is a potential vote for ethical business.

An alternative to consumption is creation. So often we consume to try to fill a gap in ourselves, yet the act of consumption often makes that gap bigger. Creation through expressing yourself is a way to fill that gap by developing self-insight and self-love. It's also a pretty effective way to fill time by creating memories.

The Freedom to Define How and Where to Work

Work is a critical expression of our personality and our being. What does where and how you work say about you? Corporations, from my experience, are full of people doing what they can do rather than what they want to do. Formal work culture can often override our personal values. Does the organization that you work for express your values, or the opposite? As with consumption, the place where you work represents more than just a paycheck. It's a vote for what you stand for as a human being.

Although we hear about "consumer activism"—i.e., consumers boycotting a brand or a company because of the way it operates with regard to (for example) human liberty or environmental protection—we hear much less about employee (or job candidate) activism. Perhaps the time has come for this kind of activism?

Exercise 13.3–Creating Value From Your Values

In this exercise you'll evaluate the fit between the demonstrated values of the organization you work for and your own values.

Step 1—Demonstrated values.

You will identify five key words that describe the demonstrated values (what we'd call character traits) of the organization you work for. What does your company stand for in practice (as opposed to what is written in glossy company brochures and on the website)? How are these values demonstrated in how decisions are made, and how the organization interacts with its staff, suppliers, customers, and the wider society?

Write down your five key words now.

Step 2—Fit with your values.

For each value on your list identify whether the value demonstrated by the company is aligned, misaligned, or neutral in terms of how it fits with your values.

Step 3—Evaluation and action.

What is the overall level of fit or mis-fit between your values and the organization's?

If there is a good fit, then what are the major positives?

If there is a mis-fit, then what action can you take to resolve this situation? If you are a leader in the organization, do you believe that this mis-fit is helping or hurting the organization? What can you do about it?

The Freedom to Participate In Community and Government

With freedom comes responsibility. A free community and government can turn into the opposite through apathy and neglect.

Democracy doesn't only happen every four years. It should happen every day through the choices and actions you make. If politicians fail to represent the people we must find (or become) new leaders.

We do not abdicate our responsibility to society when we choose a professional career. Instead, I believe that professionals in every market and in the public, private, medical, legal, and creative sectors have a specific responsibility to try to do right by society through shaping its institutions, keeping them honest (starting with the institutions inhabited by those same professionals), and by ensuring that the same institutions don't become elitist through failing to represent the interests of a broad cross-section of the people.

The Freedom of Knowledge and Discourse

Without respect, the apparent freedom of discourse online and in person is quickly hobbled. Free speech cannot be speech that is self-censored for fear of being unpopular or evoking the ire of, for example, Internet trolls. Although it is *de rigueur* in many social situations not to discuss religion or politics, where do we discuss these and other important and essential elements of society if not online and in person? I fear that we have already lost the ability and patience for reasoned and respectful debate. We are a poorer society as a result.

3. Build happiness

"There are lots of ways of being miserable, but there's only one way of being comfortable, and that is to stop running round after happiness. If you make up your mind not to be happy there's no reason why you shouldn't have a fairly good time." (Edith Wharton, *The Last Asset*).

This quote is one I saw printed in large letters on the wall of a health spa in a hotel in Split, Croatia. Darcy and I were there for a short break from our busy lives in London and the many pressing decisions we needed to make about our future. This was around the time I first asked myself the question, "What is a good life?", but at the time I phrased it as "What would a happy life for us look like in future"?

Given that I'd just spent the previous hours in the sun on a beach, I understood completely the idea of "stop running around after happiness." In fact, most of us already know how to make ourselves happy, at least for a short time.

What I didn't get at the time was the idea of being happy by "deciding not to be happy." It would take years and many hard-won life lessons for that point to become clear.

The key to this realization was in understanding the difference between intrinsic and extrinsic drivers of happiness. Intrinsic happiness comes from within as a natural part of who you are, or of the thing that you are doing. The Five Pillars all represent areas of intrinsic satisfaction. Spending time with a friend is (hopefully) intrinsically satisfying, since that is part of the nature of friendship.

Other potential sources of happiness, such as money or flashy possessions, are extrinsic, since they don't contain happiness within themselves, but rely on an external factor for their power. Often this factor is *social comparison* (i.e., comparing oneself to other people).

For example, you buy a new car, and then your neighbor buys the latest redesigned model. Suddenly your new car no longer has the same power as a status symbol, even though it looks the same as it did the day before.

We stay on track to a good life by having the courage to escape the idea of happiness defined only in extrinsic terms.

For most of my life I thought about happiness as a thing, trying to fill up a bucket of happiness through pleasure and experiences. Many of us try to fill our happiness bucket through success or possessions. Happiness is a "thing," but in a non-material sense. It is a feeling. You can't bottle feelings, or fill a bucket with them. They come and go.

Instead, the insight that I eventually achieved was that happiness is an outcome of a specific philosophy, process, and practice of living. It is the outcome of a life that we actively create, just as balance and meaning are. The key to sustained happiness is not chasing an ephemeral feeling again and again, but creating a life that produces a foundation for long-lasting happiness.

By being clear on who you are, loving yourself, and being resourceful in how best to create value, it's quite possible to live a good life and yet still have a nice material existence, too—so long as you approach things in that order.

Framing the question I asked on the beach that day in terms of "happiness" rather than a "good life" set me on the wrong track, and probably made my search for a good life a quest rather than simply a process (a process that I hope that you can follow in this book, in less time than it took me). It took years and several life events for me to realize that we need a definition of what we ultimately strive for that is holistic (happiness, balance, and meaning) and connected (love, hope, and compassion).

While happiness is an important ingredient of a satisfying life, it is not the whole of life. If we only ever did things that made us happy in the moment then it's unlikely that we'd ever achieve much of anything worthwhile (who would go to the gym, or study, or write a book?).

It is probably not a stretch to say that few of humankind's greatest achievements would ever have been realized if we as a human race were solely happiness-seekers, though somehow we as a society have elevated happiness to the highest pedestal in what we seek from life.

We stay on track to a good life by having the courage to escape the definition of happiness as a material thing, and recognize instead that *happiness is who we are.*

Exercise 13.4—Sustained Happiness

Step 1—Sources of happiness.

List three examples of intrinsic happiness in your life and three examples of extrinsic happiness.

Step 2—Evaluation.

How do your sources of intrinsic happiness differ from the extrinsic ones, in terms of how they make you feel? How is the happiness you feel from each different?

Step 3—Increasing intrinsic happiness.

Identify one action that you can take in the next week to take time spent pursuing an extrinsic activity and use it to focus on an intrinsic one instead.

If you haven't already, how can you make a habit of including more sources of intrinsic happiness in your typical week?

In my quest I've found that there are two types of regrets. The first is not doing what you know is right. The second is not sacrificing to do the right things in the right way when it really matters. Our regrets often stem from chasing success based on extrinsic measures of happiness rather than what we know in our heart to be right.

NOTES

CHAPTER 14
Maintaining A Sense Of Humor

Regressing, processing, what am I doing here?
I suspend disbelief
Now to my relief I see an answer clear

We're all dancing to the rhythm of our planet
My dial was knocked - so all I got was static

From up high I see a sight
The endless cycle of day and night
That last year is still here
. . . and tomorrow here too

Lost time is found
It has always been around
to no-one, just me, I proclaim
that life is but a game!

-excerpt from "Rum, Tum-tum" by Brett Cowell

This chapter makes the case that retaining your sense of humor toward this business of life is essential to achieving your potential.

In fact, humor cuts across the themes—perspective, connection and courage—covered to this point in Part Two. You can even find humor as part of Contribution. This is because humor and humility are so often linked.

When times are tough it can pay to believe that there will be good times in the future. Humor can be a great stress reliever. Being overly serious can limit how we see the world, narrowing our consciousness to such an extent that we can stop seeing the possibility for joy and lighter times in life.

Humor can be a way to connect honestly with the world around us, particularly the self-deprecating kind of humor which, if done with heart, can be an example of self-love. This type of humor means not being blind to either your strengths or your weaknesses, but using the knowledge of both to allow yourself to take a breath and continue on your path of personal change.

Believe it or not, humor is also an essential ingredient in courage. If you thought about every possible thing that could go wrong, even in moving towards something positive such as a good life, then you'd never do anything. Perfectionism is often a humorless trait, and it certainly isn't a very pragmatic one for *starting* toward the achievement of anything significant in the world. Start first, then seek increased quality as you settle into your journey. *Aiming for perfection from the get-go means that you'll never start or finish anything.* Laugh at your mistakes and wrong turns and be glad of the opportunity to learn from them. Those who depend on you would rather have a piece of something than a whole lot of nothing. That's been my experience, anyway.

Exercise 14.1—Humor

When was the last time you laughed (at home and at work)?

When you did your lifeline exercise, did you find that there were both ups *and* downs? How can that insight allow you to let more light into your life?

Identify one particularly difficult area of your life right now. What is funny (or at least darkly comedic) about it? Or is there something about it that illustrates the truth that we're all just fallible humans? From a place of light, how can you reframe that situation in a way that allows you space to breathe?

NOTES

CHAPTER 15
Making a Larger Contribution

Reaching your potential may not be about what you do for you at all, but the contribution you make to others.

Culturally, I think most of us get the idea of success followed by contribution. We see the example of billionaire philanthropists, and perhaps this reinforces the idea that the correct path through life is to accumulate as much money as possible and then do something worthwhile. Perhaps a more helpful way to look at the same situation is that people who have the wealth and leisure to do anything often choose contribution. Why wait?

What if you could apply the confidence gained from making changes in your life to a wider community? What if making changes for others gave you the confidence to change yourself? In my case performing skills-based volunteering with a charity focused on social entrepreneurship gave me a concrete experience that I could use to reorient what I believed about the world and myself. It gave me access to a new plane of possibilities within myself.

Perhaps you're already looking at global issues and thinking: could I or should I try to do something about them? Or perhaps you're just wondering what business of yours these issues are.

As a professional you have significant resources available to help others—not only financial, but relationships, skills you possess, the ability to communicate in an impactful way, the ability to influence your organization and other organizations. At the same time you may experience several obstacles to helping others.

You might believe that time is a constraint. That you simply don't have time to help others. You might be fearful that although successful in your career, you won't be as successful in helping others.

You might simply believe that helping is too much trouble.

Helping others involves allocating time wisely, and also experimenting with different approaches to helping until you find the one or ones that most resonate with you and are most effective for those you are trying to help.

Let's have a brief look at eight different types of helping. Many of these overlap—the idea of spelling out all eight of them is to help stimulate your thinking.

They are:

- Helping those in your circle
- Mentoring others
- Creating a positive work environment
- Donations and volunteering

- Skills-based volunteering
- Business social value
- Social entrepreneurship
- Social involvement and community engagement

There is no prescriptive way to pick which area to help in, so you should probably start in an area that you have an affinity for. If you like food, then you could pick a food-based giving exercise; if you like sports, then perhaps this is an area you can find or create a giving opportunity in; if you spend time hiking or scuba diving then helping to preserve the environment in which these activities take place could be an area for you to be involved in. Almost certainly there are those who can benefit from your professional and leadership skills and interests. As you start to garner some initial wins, you can extend your efforts to other areas.

Helping Those In Your Circle

Perhaps others have projects that they are working on that you can directly help with—possibly by reviewing their approach. Perhaps there are those at work who could benefit from this book, or some of the concepts in it? A book club or action group format can be an effective way to help create a good life for your circle and to magnify the positive effects for others.

If "charity begins at home" then remember that at its root charity is love! Are you showing love and compassion to those in your life? Can you be an inspiration to them, a role model?

Sometimes the path to more elaborate and impactful ways of helping can start with really listening to another person (or people) and trying to connect with them as fellow human beings.

Mentoring Others

Helping others can extend to your circle at work, including mentoring and teaching others. Mentoring is often said to be one of the most transformational of personal relationships for both mentee and mentor.

Some organizations already have a mentor program of some kind. Would it make sense for you to engage with that program? Are there people inside or outside your organization whom you could mentor?

The mentor relationship is also something that you should pursue with adequate care—by not taking on too many mentees, and by setting expectations upfront around availability, expectations, and confidentiality of the mentoring relationship.

Creating A Positive Work Environment

You have a role as a manager and a team member to create a positive work environment. This is not about being cheery and wishing everyone a good day, though that probably wouldn't hurt. Instead, it's more about creating opportunities for people to develop in a merit-based and flexible working environment.

You support a merit-based environment by offering 360-degree feedback, and being clear on the behaviors and values that your organization supports. Delegating effectively is also a practical step to creating a positive work environment for your team.

Supporting a flexible work environment goes beyond the policy—it's about encouraging and role-modeling effective, flexible work options. Although this is under the heading of helping others, it makes perfect business sense too, particularly if your organization strives to attract and retain the best people.

Donations and Volunteering

Donations are one of the most widespread and well known forms of giving. There are many avenues to support charity through donations, including fundraising and sponsorship-based events, e.g., fun-runs, etc.

You can also get creative with giving—it is becoming increasingly common for people to request a donation to a charity instead of a gift for themselves. You may also decide to link the achievement of goals in your personal project to donations to charity.

Volunteering is also a widespread mechanism for giving. This could range from participating in corporate charity day to donating time and money to personal causes or faith-based programs.

Many people report that volunteering has changed their lives. They expected to go into volunteering in order to give something, and yet they got more out of it, and in unexpected ways. The instant antidote to any preconceptions you may have about others is, often, simply meeting and working with people from different backgrounds and with levels of opportunity different than your own.

Skills-Based Volunteering

While most traditional volunteering is in helping to deliver front-line services, skills-based volunteering is focused on improving the processes, strategy, marketing or performance measures of the charity or cause (i.e., linking what the charity does to actual measurable outcomes in the community).

As professionals we have the opportunity to multiply the impact of an hour's worth of volunteering by helping the charity or cause to make systematic improvements in its business or field operations. These operational changes continue to deliver benefits long after the hours of work are done.

Your role could be to get directly involved, or to at least be aware of the existence of this type of volunteering, and to see if there are opportunities for your organization to pilot a program with a local charity. Volunteering options no longer have to include just things like landscaping at the local school—employees should have the opportunity to become involved in traditional and skills-based volunteering.

The benefits for individuals include sharpening of skills, increased work satisfaction and employee retention, not to mention the ability to build wider relationships in the community (which may in turn translate into business opportunities).

Business Social Value

It is a common misconception that any giving that an organization does must necessarily reduce its own bottom line. My experience is that this doesn't have to be the case.

As you've just read, skills-based volunteering can offer the individual personal and professional development opportunities that more than repay the hours put in. How could this principle apply to a whole organization? Well, firstly, the net effect across the organization of a widespread skills-based volunteering program could be a significant increase in employee engagement and morale . . . something that many organizations would like to buy "off the shelf" from any source if it were available.

But there is a larger opportunity here. Businesses exist in a wider social context, and the list of stakeholders and environmental factors that large organizations must manage is increasing. These stakeholders/drivers include: increasing regulation, customer and shareholder activism, and supply constraints on everything from water to energy.

In fact, my experience has been that what is valuable for business and what is valuable to society are NOT always mutually exclusive. The picture looks more like two intersecting circles, with so-called business social value at the overlap. A simple example would be improving logistics efficiency, which saves on fuel costs *and* reduces greenhouse gas emissions.

Most large organizations are running too many projects, with some of those projects using up resources for little or even negative overall returns. I think there is an opportunity for large organizations to add some business social value projects to their overall portfolio. As with personal experimentation, these small projects can often yield unexpected, positive results beyond what they set out to do.

Approaching positive business and social change from inside the organization can be difficult, and you could meet with resistance and inertia based on a desire to maintain the status quo. Perhaps your stakeholders in the organization just need a little time to see the benefits of working in a different way. You'll need patience, tenacity, and the ability to apply a flexible approach—many of the qualities required of an entrepreneur. This is why professionals who pursue changes from within organizations are sometimes called social "intrapreneurs".

Social Entrepreneurship

Social entrepreneurship (also sometimes referred to as social business) is a business that devotes a material amount of its profit and/or purpose to social aims. Imagine a business model of a self-funding charity that generates its income from the sale of products or services, and you begin to get a perspective of the power of social entrepreneurship.

In my experience, the prevalence of this kind of model varies greatly across the world, as does the depth, maturity, and success of the social business approach as a whole. While good examples of social business models exist in narrow sectors, a more widespread blueprint for successful social enterprise is still in its infancy.

Businesses pursuing a social entrepreneurship model (particularly at start-up and scaling stages) can benefit from the type of skills that the professionals reading this book possess. Working with local social enterprises can be a rewarding application of the skills-based volunteering/coaching concept, and can help to develop new social models that can be shared with others to magnify the impact of the work.

Social Involvement Or Community Engagement

The definition of social involvement is very broad, but at its heart is the pursuit of a cause that has a direct, positive impact on society. This could be anything from taking an interest in the preservation of your local park or river to being on a school or charity board, or consumer activism, or helping to solve world hunger. It could mean trying to contribute to a better society through politics at all levels.

WHY DO THIS?

Part of the reason is as simple as this: to make a contribution bigger than yourself. You could start with a heartfelt calling; you could get angry or frustrated at a specific situation; or you could get drawn into social involvement through an issue that affects you directly.

I believe that you can also gravitate to a cause in the wider search for meaning in your life. Dedicating a chunk of your time to the pursuit of making the world a slightly better place is gratifying and feels worthwhile. If this sounds good but you still don't know where to start, then start small and start locally, but start.

Our modern lives are driving us to become more individualistic and to forget our common humanity. All of the approaches described in this chapter are ways to regain our humanity.

※ ※ ※

Our real potential exists beyond what we can see and any vision that we can set for ourselves today. When we've reached our vision, the world doesn't stop. We see the world in a different way. We have more experience and often more resources, at least in terms of people that we interact with. If our initial vision was bold enough, we may have also uncovered a life purpose on the way to achieving the vision. The life purpose will provide additional depth and focus for the creation of your next vision.

The potential I'm interested in with respect to myself is that which goes beyond the vision that you read about in Chapter 3.

This potential relates to how I can get the ideas in *The Good Life Book* out to more people, so that it takes hold and becomes more than just another chapter in my life story. It becomes one small part of creating a better society and a better world.

If you started Part Two not seeing the possibility or hope of a better life for yourself, then I hope that you ended it with a renewed sense of the infinite potential that we all have access to. This potential is something that we must hold on to if our path to a better life becomes a difficult one, as is sometimes the case. Otherwise we risk becoming derailed.

The barriers to a good life are common amongst humans, and often they are *comfortable* too. We put up walls out of fear, to prevent ourselves from failing or being hurt, or by feeling that we aren't good enough. These walls become a prison, an *un*-comfort zone that leads to regret. Instead of walls, be like water—flowing and expansive.

PART THREE
GETTING THERE

Once I was alive
Things were ahead of me
Always just ahead of me

Back then I thought I'd live forever
But I never did.

"Life is what happens when you're making other plans" (said JL)
Yet I made few demands
It was in my hands. I suppose

If dreams were currency I'd be a rich man,
Still, "You can't take them with you"
That I probably knew

Time is vast, but it went fast
I never did today, at last, I guess
Just whatever I could do, a start

And now it's clear, it's true, the games up, my time is through.
Regrets a few, no redo is due. All done.

This tale is told as best I can
I hope you'll live a better one
A life that's fresh and full and new.

What happens next is down to you.

Once I was Alive (the day I died).

The final part of this book is dedicated to *getting there*, or in other words to growth through taking action. Let's return to the travel guide metaphor from the start of the book. You've read the guide and decided where you want to go. You've even travelled there in your mind already, seeing yourself at the destination, and gotten your head around going to somewhere new. Now it's time to schedule the trip and buy the tickets.

Getting there is about setting you up for success in your personal change—not only through the right structured approach, tools and techniques, but also the right expectations and attitude to change.

It's important that as we move into the nuts and bolts of change that you keep in mind the magic and wonder of your vision for a good life. As you are taking a thousand steps to a good life, remember where you're going and why you're going there

As the old song goes "It's not [just] what you do, it's the way that you do it." How will you bring your personal flair and expression to everything that you are doing in order to live a good life? If you can do that, then you are already starting to live a life that is good.

CHAPTER 16
Taking Action

Personal change comes in different shapes and sizes, and it progresses in different ways. Your path to a better life could be smooth and incremental, or crashing and transformative. The place that you start from could be in the depths of crisis, or with a fairly good life that you wish to make better. The next step in your good life journey could take weeks, months, or possibly years. No matter the scale, mode, or timeframe of your change, you'll likely have to complete the change before you are completely comfortable with it. I only began to feel truly comfortable with the decision to change up my vocational portfolio around six months *after* I finished up at my corporate consulting job. This was the case even although the recognition of the need to change happened years before I began the process.

The stakes surrounding your ability to change or your failure to change in terms of living a good life are high—for yourself, your family, your community and perhaps even the world. Yet how do we take a positive step before our fear stops us from acting? If the change we are attempting is complex or will take a long time, then how do we manage it most effectively, in order to increase the chance of success? These are the questions that I'll attempt to provide detailed answers to in this and the following two chapters.

I hope that this book will be a trigger for you to change your life in a positive way. The need to change, to grow and then maintain a good life is something that I believe will be relevant to you not only on this initial journey, but also for the rest of your life. Because we need to continue to grow throughout our lives, Part Three is supported by a number of skills and techniques grouped under the discipline of Enabling Growth (represented by the tree symbol). To grow, a tree needs energy from the Sun (Part One) and water and nutrients from the Earth (Part Two). This metaphorical linkage between the three disciplines that underlie the book (Directing Energy, Unlocking Potential, and Enabling Growth) is intentional, designed to represent a "cycle of life" and, as well, something to ponder as you form your own philosophy of what a good life is.

Given the different types of change that we might need to make during our lives, I want to introduce a simple framework for taking action by using the acronym DEEP, or Decisions, Experiences, Experiments, and Projects. Once you recognize the need to grow, you can select the most appropriate method of the four to help you do so.

DECISIONS

In most cases, when I undertake a strategic project for a consulting client, many of the ideas of what needs to change are already on the table, and perhaps have already been looked at many times before but not implemented (or not implemented successfully). Part of what is missing, assuming a strategy can be put in place, is the ability on the organization's part to translate the strategy into a concise analysis of what actually needs to change (and therefore what decisions are required) and then develop a consistent set of criteria for making decisions.

The quickest and simplest way to change your life in a positive way is to make a positive decision. Often in our lives we know what we need to do in order to make a change, but we hesitate or procrastinate around the decision to take action. One of the reasons we do this is, of course, fear. Fear of making the wrong decision or of cutting off options. Good, old-fashioned fear of failure.

The journey that you've been on so far was designed in a way that leads you to a place of being able to begin to identify some of the key decisions that you need to make in order to live a good life, and then to make them.

You've identified an overall direction for your life. Assessing whether a decision would bring you closer to your vision and is aligned with your life direction can help you to make the decision. You've defined good in each key pillar of your life. Will your decision lead to a balanced definition of good in your life? You've read about strategic choices. Are you struggling to make a decision because you have the wrong choices (bigger "bets") in place? You've read about internal obstacles to change that can derail you. Are you failing to make a decision that is good for you in life because it would take you beyond the realm of your current identity or professional job? You've defined your burning platform. Were you unable to make a decision because you didn't understand the compelling reason to do so, including the negative consequences you may suffer from not deciding?

The choice embodied by the prioritization of your pillars that you performed in Chapter 10 should have brought to a head some key decisions in your life.

For example, one of the most powerful decisions you can make is to use the prioritization of your five pillars as the way that you'll really make day-to-day decisions.

The implication, for me, of the choice to prioritize family above vocation is that this book has taken a greater number of months to write than if I'd locked myself away in a secluded writing space for the whole time. I made decisions based on this choice again and again. That I was not prepared to miss meal and bath times with my kids, or their awake time on weekends, or the precious quiet time with my wife (after the kids have gone to bed). These decisions (and the overall choice) came with the risk that I would run out of time and not finish this writing project at all.

In *your* life, if you stick with your prioritization of pillars and the decisions that go along with that, you may miss out on, for example, a promotion, or lose friends that liked "the old you." This may be the price of achieving an overall life that is good for you, and minimizes regret. Making a decision usually lifts a huge weight off our shoulders. Making the decision probably won't feel comfortable at the time (or perhaps for some time afterwards) but it is a way to convert unproductive anxiety (worrying) into productive anxiety (trying to make your decision work).

Exercise 16.1–Decisions

In this exercise you'll identify key decisions that you can make to help you progress to your definition of a good life.

Step 1—Create list of decisions.

Using your notes from Part One and Part Two, create a list of no more than ten decisions that you could make that are relevant to your path to a good life.

Step 2—Evaluate decisions.

From the list you've created, rank the decisions in terms of the scale of benefit you'd expect from making each one, and then also assess how much effort would be involved in making the decision: is it easy (you can decide today) or hard (you would require more information on what the decision would entail)?

Step 3—Identify key decisions.

From your list you will identify your top three decisions, selecting at least one that would make a noticeable difference to your life and that you could also decide to do today (even if the actions relating to the decision may take more time).

You will also note down your estimate of the benefits in life that you'll get from making the decision. This will help push you to make the decision.

Sometimes it is easiest to understand the benefits of making a decision by evaluating the long-term impact of what would happen if you continued to *not* make that decision. For example, the benefit of a single gym workout on your overall health probably won't convince you to work out. However, if you continually decide not to improve your fitness you may suffer long-term health consequences, have less energy at work, not achieve your life goals, not be the person you want to be and so on.

Identify your key decisions and the benefits you'll get (or negative consequences you'll avoid) by making them.

Step 4—Plan and decide.

List the steps you'd have to take, including information gathering, experiences and experiments (described in the next two sections) that will provide additional context and evidence to support your decisions.

Understand which elements of the work you've done in Parts One or Two provide useful context that can help you make the decision (i.e., your overall direction, definition of good, internal obstacles, choices, etc.).

At a minimum, identify one *concrete step* you can take toward making the bigger decision, and decide now to take that step.

Make your decision(s) now.

EXPERIENCES

New experiences can help us see the world in a different way and achieve our goals, even if the experience is sometimes not directly related to the goal. Our experiences can define us, so having a new or uncommon experience can help to "unstick" you in life.

The reason why this works is that we often close ourselves up, for example due to the obstacles you heard about in Part Two. Having a new experience provides both new and diverse input to your field of possibilities, and also stretches your comfort zone. Even such a small change as trying a new restaurant, or reading your copy of *The Good Life Book* in a place that you don't normally sit in (e.g., your local library) can reduce your resistance to making other, larger changes.

The next step in your good life journey could be simply to try something new.

If so, what would that experience be?

EXPERIMENTS

During my consulting career I, like many professionals and leaders, tended to frame issues relating to my personal goals and challenges as requiring an all-or-nothing rather than a trial-and-error or incremental effort.

The difficulty with this all-or-nothing mindset is that the unknowns in such a big effort are many, and often sufficient to stop us from doing anything at all. This is the antithesis of a portfolio approach—we put all our eggs (energy) in one basket, rather than generating and exploring a range of options. Using the all-or-nothing approach in the pursuit of happiness is ineffective, since the stark truth is that we often don't know at the start of our journey what will make us truly happy over the longer term, or the best way to reach whatever our goal may be.

An experiment is simply a structured way of trying things that lets us explore, engage and evaluate different ways of achieving our goals, and in a relatively quick and painless way, before scaling up our level of commitment. Keeping things small allows you to get started more quickly. If your goal is to change jobs or alter your vocational portfolio, then an experimental approach can allow you to understand, try out and refine potential changes while keeping the security of your current job.

The exploring aspect of an experiment is a way to understand and experience the different characteristics or categories and the scope of whatever you are trying to do.

If your goal is to lose weight, then exploring this goal would reveal that the categories of doing this include diet, exercise, or even surgery. Within the categories of diet, exercise, and surgery there are different approaches to achieving the goal. For example, to exercise you could go to the gym, run, ride a bike, play a sport and so on. While surgery is in fact a way that people use to lose weight, I mentioned it as a provocative way to get you to challenge your assumptions on how to achieve any goal. Sometimes evaluating options that initially appear "out of left field" can be an effective way to find the best overall solution, even if it turns out not to be the left field one. Almost always left field options will provide insights that let you see the problem in a different light.

The "engage" part of the experiment is to try the different options and see which one works best. A key in exploration is that each avenue that you explore should have a low impact or be reversible if the experiment fails. For this reason you may choose not to engage with the surgery solution, or instead to engage by speaking with people who have had such surgery. Speaking to another person who has attempted whatever change you may be considering gives you more than just simple facts. In addition, you obtain insights into the emotional and psychological background of the change.

Instead of having to try all the options in order to reach your goal, most experiments will instead begin with a hypothesis. A hypothesis in this context is a statement about the solution or approach that you believe to be true based on past experience, or on research. You could research why people prefer one method of fitness over another, which would allow you to understand the criteria people use to select that choice. For example, many people find that socialization with others is the key part of what makes team sports an attractive fitness option. If you are a social person (or want to be) then you could form a hypothesis that finding a team sport is where you need to start.

You could then run an experiment to try touch-rugby after work, and after trying it you can evaluate how effectively it met your criteria of increasing fitness while also being social. What worked and what didn't in your experiment will inform your next steps. For example, if you found that socialization was a critical element of what works for you in fitness, but that you didn't like rugby, then you could try group cycling or running and so on. In order to decide which team sport or activity to try next you could find out why people like running or cycling and then form your next hypothesis based on how well those reasons match what is important to you.

An experiment can be used to scan a range of options, find a single workable solution, or do a side-by-side comparison of known options.

An experiment gets you to engage with your goal. Before engaging it's hard to understand the true nature of what you're trying to do. An experience, even one that is not perfect, will tell you more in a short time than you could find out at your desk.

For example, before I attended my first storytellers and poets group open mic, I believed that the outcome would be determined only by the quality of the words I'd written in advance. After the first time I attended and robotically stumbled through my reading, I discovered that the performance aspect was equally if not more important to the overall outcome (entertaining people) than the words I'd written.

Later I found that the process of preparing, performing, and reviewing gave me confidence to use the same approach in other activities that had nothing to do with writing. Engaging allows you to understand unexpected positive and negative side effects related to the thing that you're trying to do.

The final part of an experiment is evaluation. Although evaluation is the final step, you should identify some criteria before running the experiment so that you know whether it has been a success or not. In the fitness example your experimental criteria could include how effectively the activity is helping you to lose weight, whether you like doing the activity, is it social and so on.

Although, for simple experiments, whether they worked or not may be self-evident, applying a bit more discipline can help you to get to the best solution. This may be as simple as, for example, researching what criteria others have used to assess the same activity that you will be experimenting with. For example, what I like about cycling rather than running is that I get to explore more (cover more distance) and to think more creatively. In contrast, when I'm running I'm mainly thinking about wishing I had bigger lungs.

If your goal is more complex, such as exploring the idea of starting a new business, then it's critical that you build in more structure for finding assessment criteria for your experiment, and then accurately measuring the results.

Exercise 16.2—Experiment

In this exercise you'll design a simple experiment for one of your goals.

Step 1—Select a goal.

Identify a life goal that you can't yet easily see how to achieve.

Step 2—Design an experiment.

Are you seeking to explore a range of completely different areas, to evaluate options in a specific area, or to test out an approach to a goal? If the answer is some combination of the above, then you might want to split the experiment into several smaller ones.

Document your objectives for the experiment, your approach and how you will measure success.

Step 3—Run the experiment.

Try running your experiment by taking action. Remember to document your observations at various stages of the experiment.

For small experiments you may want to repeat the experiment a couple of times. Sometimes the newness of what we're trying to do overwhelms the ability to get a true sense of what we're doing (due to nerves perhaps, or having an off day). For example, if you're assessing a gym, you may go at different times of the day, or try different programs before deciding whether gyms are for you. Experiments relating to a change of habits often have to be run over a period of weeks to get a true indication of whether your selected approach to the change works.

Step 4—Evaluate results.

When the experiment is at an appropriate stage, evaluate progress against the criteria that you set up when you designed the experiment. Don't forget to document any unexpected aspects of what you learn from the experiment.

Step 5—Next steps.

Decide what comes next. If the experiment was a success against the experimental criteria, does it support making a firm decision or scaling the experiment up to a project?

If the experiment did not achieve the objectives you had set for it, then work out what has to change in your next experiment's design.

A more formalized approach to managing the work associated with a personal change is to create a personal project.

PROJECTS

A project is a way to describe and organize activities in order to produce a specific output or outputs in support of one or more outcomes.

You could create a personal project to train for and run a marathon, or to write your own cookbook, or to help homeless kids through a charity.

Even without applying the more detailed project management techniques that you'll hear about shortly, you can increase the likelihood of achieving a positive outcome in your life by calling what you're trying to achieve a project, rather than simply a goal. A personal project has an identity separate from you. When you try to achieve a goal and things don't work out straight away, it's easy to take it personally, and even be defensive toward those who may try to help you.

Even so, some of the goals we seek to achieve, such as the ones mentioned at the start of this section, are more complex, since they involve a series of interdependent activities or "moving parts" and may take weeks or months to complete.

These types of projects can often benefit from a higher degree of organization and structure in order to increase the chances of success. Most of us won't be quitting our job to plan or do our projects, but will need an effective way to be able to pick up and put down our project as we deal with our other commitments. This additional level of guidance will be provided in the next chapters. For now I'll describe three elements of a project: outputs, activities, and timeline.

Every project must have a written-down set of outputs. These outputs could include a list of objectives that the project seeks to achieve (e.g., a successfully run marathon) and also tangible products the project will deliver (e.g., a finished cookbook, if that was your project). The project outputs should be described in enough detail so that you can actually measure whether the project has been successful. Often the success of the project will be determined before you start by how clearly you can visualize what the results of the project will be. However, the project outputs shouldn't describe every step of how to complete the project. You may have to try several approaches or undergo several course adjustments as you progress in order to deliver the outputs.

Having clear outputs that you can visualize is one reason why it doesn't make sense to undertake a project that includes changing jobs, losing weight, and finding a new hobby. It is best to split these into three separate projects so that each can have clear outputs and a clear set of actions, and so that you can avoid taking on too much or losing sight of what you set out to achieve in the first place.

Activities. A project breaks down an output or objective into a series of smaller steps or activities, and then these steps are ordered in a logical sequence. There may be several different approaches (with different sets of activities) that you could use to achieve the project's outputs. Your experience and any research you do on similar projects undertaken by others will point you toward a specific approach for starting your project. As you get into the project you may need to refine or change the approach if you are executing the individual steps well but nevertheless get off the track to achieving your project's objectives.

The final core component of a project is a timeline. The timeline is defined either "top-down" by starting with a set timeframe and then apportioning that time to individual activities, or "bottom-up" where you add up the time estimates for individual activities to come up with the overall timeline.

Writing down the three components of outputs, activities, and timelines provides the minimum amount of structure required to enable tracking of the project on a periodic basis. Most projects (even professionally run ones) often get off track at one point or another, and therefore having a weekly tracking point, for example, allows you to determine if the project is off track and, if so, to take corrective action.

Personal projects often encompass elements of the other three avenues for growth (Decisions, Experiences, and Experiments), and roll these into the more formalized project structure. For example, one of the agenda items in your weekly project review could be decisions to be made, or ideas for experiences or experiments that would further help to refine the project approach or outputs.

In the next chapter you will work on identification of your personal project or portfolio.

WRAP-UP

In this chapter you've heard about four paths to enable growth—through Decisions, Experiences, Experiments, and Projects. Whether you choose one or a combination of these, please do not move beyond this chapter without selecting at least one of them to put into practice.

Whichever form of action you decide to try out, I've found that it is most effective to designate a dedicated time each week to review the progress of your project against your plan, and to review and update your list of actions.

Sunday evening or first thing Monday morning can be an effective time to do this. Even as you are working through this book, deciding which project to do, or after completing an experiment or project, it can make sense to get into the habit of using a set time each week to review your progress toward a better life. You can review your Five Pillars or even just how you feel and why. With practice, your good life review can become a habit that you can complete at different times during the week and in just a few minutes, e.g., while waiting for a coffee or for a meeting to start.

NOTES

CHAPTER 17
Getting REAL

By its nature the path of personal change is rarely a straight line. A sailing metaphor comes readily to mind. We zigzag toward our goal, with progress dependent on the conditions that surround us. Sometimes the wind is at our backs and we speed forward. At other times we face a headwind or no wind at all, and stall in our efforts, or even drift backwards. This sailing metaphor is not perfect, since our perspective changes the moment we embark on a change. Our viewpoint changes, our focus (what we prioritize) changes and, through openness, who we are changes.

The best type of change, and perhaps the only effective kind, is honest change. Growth is often not glamorous. It often doesn't feel good during every moment involved in making the change. But you *are* in the moment and doing it. That is the most important thing.

Shortly you'll do an exercise to help select your project or portfolio, then hear about two approaches: REAL and Plan, Do, Review. Both of them can help you start and manage your projects.

Exercise 17.1–Project or Portfolio

Step 1—Identify candidate project(s).

Write down a list of any potential projects that you've identified so far.

Even if you haven't thought about your opportunities in project terms, answer the following question: Which specific parts of my life contain the largest problems or opportunities?

Step 2—Rank opportunities.

Rank your projects (or life opportunity areas) in terms of the return they give, using whatever metrics you have, or in terms of ROLE (Return On Life Energy). To do this, think specifically about what problem(s) the project will solve.

Next, rank the projects in terms of urgency.

Based on the returns and urgency, which three seem to offer the biggest opportunities?

Step 3—Document project outputs.

For the highest opportunity project, write a short statement that summarizes the project objectives and what outputs or outcomes the project will deliver.

You will continue with this same project for the purposes of completing this exercise, and can return to use the same approach for ranking your other projects or opportunity areas.

Step 4—Identify key activities.

Given the outputs and objectives of the project, create a list of key activities (groups of steps) that you'd have to perform to complete the project.

If possible, write down detailed steps under each activity. Refining this list of steps is likely to take a couple of attempts, so do the best you can now, and be prepared to return later, rather than not write anything.

Step 5—Determine provisional timeline.

Based on the activities that you've identified, what is the provisional timeline for the project?

Step 6—Your portfolio.

Based on your identified project(s) and other opportunities in your life, is there an obvious first grouping of project(s) and opportunities that could form the basis of your portfolio?

Remember that a portfolio is a way to manage a group of activities that you want to work on over time. Don't take on too much at once! Try to ensure that you don't combine too many disparate and unrelated objectives into a project just purely because you plan to do those activities in the same time period. It's better to split a project into several smaller projects with clear objectives and then use your portfolio to determine how and when to start those smaller projects (i.e., using prioritization criteria such as the ROLE of each project).

MAKING IT *REAL*

I want to share with you a great approach for bringing your dreams to life. It's called REAL, or Ruminate, Excuses, Avoid, and Lie to yourself. Oh wait! That's not it. This version of REAL is not what should happen, but what often does happen. Despite our initial enthusiasm for making a change, and the obvious, logical reasons for doing so, many personal change efforts fail. Rumination is one of the biggest reasons. We get stuck, turning what we want to do over and over in our mind. Even if we try something, we may find that it doesn't solve all of our problems overnight, so we go back to the thinking stage.

Excuses are what come next; we say to ourselves that it's not the right time, or that we are not meant to be successful. Avoidance is the next step. We procrastinate or do other things that distract us from having to engage in any way in what we're trying to achieve. This reinforces the view that the project has stalled or doesn't work. The last step is lying to ourselves. We convince ourselves that what we aim to do was always a bad idea anyway, and it's is best to put it behind us. Doesn't sound great—but does it sound familiar?

A more productive definition of REAL is Research, Engage, Analyze, and Learn. Researching, rather than mindlessly surfing the Internet, is focused on understanding the scale and scope of, and possible approaches to what you're trying to do, and identifying some people who can help you to do it. Although books can be useful resources, I've found that it's often better to allocate a fixed amount of time, e.g., two hours, for Internet research to answer the following questions:

Scale—how easy or difficult is what you're trying to do? How long does it take a beginner to achieve the goal/become proficient at the activity? What is the cheapest way to engage in the activity for three months (i.e., a period long enough to enable you to determine next steps)?

Scope—what are the different "flavors" or categories of the thing you're trying to do? For example, even running has different distances, city vs. off road, solo vs. group runs, etc. If you are trying to do something new you may not even be aware of the different categories, some of which may be more appealing to you than any that you were aware of before doing the research

Approach—what are the typical approaches people use to achieve the goal? What are the key tips and tricks for ensuring success?

People—who are the people that you could engage with, either online or in your local area, in order to get help?

Your research should give you some concrete ideas of how to *engage* with your goal. The best way to engage is to seek or create an experience or experiment that lets you understand the nature of your goal directly. You can seek out people who are doing or have done what you want to do, and then contact them.

Next, analyze the results of what you've done, and what you must do next. Each time you run through a cycle of REAL you should be able to answer the question of "so what?" relating to what you just did. How will the information you've read or collected benefit you in planning or in executing what you do in a more effective way? This "so what" technique is one that I now automatically use when I'm drawn to read an article online or elsewhere. The article may be pleasant to read or well written, but so what—if I'm not taking anything tangible away then it's probably time to stop reading it.

Finally, as part of the REAL cycle, ensure that you summarize what you've learned from your actions so far. The discipline of REAL is that it trains you to always be taking one more step forward toward your goal. Documenting what you learn is a way of applying the information you collect to your own personal situation. It allows you to learn effectively from the experiences of others since you can answer "what does that mean to me"? and "what do I need to do differently as a result of this information"?

The next chapter describes a detailed approach to managing a personal project.

CHAPTER 18
Planning, Doing, Reviewing

OVERVIEW

Although creating a project can be an effective way to plan and organize work, many projects still fail.

Common reasons for failure include:

- Benefits of doing the project are unclear
- Unrealistic expectations of what the project can achieve
- Scope or complexity of project too great (at commencement, or over time)
- Project objectives unclear
- Project timeline, risks, and issues are not managed
- Transition at end of project not managed
- No plan in place to get or sustain benefits of project

These reasons shouldn't put you off doing a project. Rather, they should reinforce why having a structured approach to your project can be useful. I've been exposed to numerous project management methodologies and performance improvement approaches during my time as a management consultant. Despite the number and variety of possible approaches, I've found that the best approach to anything is the one that is simplest to understand and therefore the one that you actually use.

Given this, I want to share the most fundamental of all approaches to change, the action cycle of *plan, do,* and *review*.

Figure 18.1 – "Plan, Do, Review" Cycle

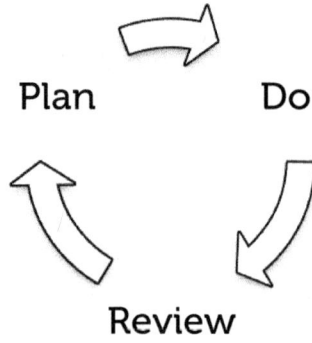

First we plan and prepare for a change, then take action (do), and finally we review what we did in terms of what happened and whether it met our expectations. In the review stage we also identify any corrective actions for the next cycle.

The plan, do, review cycle can be used for individual actions, and I have also created a version that you can use for managing an entire project.

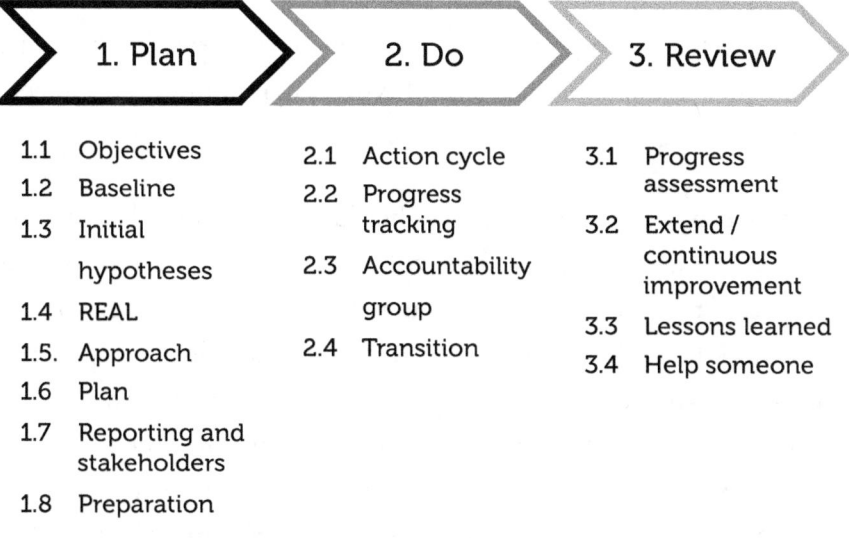

Figure 18.2 – "Plan, Do, Review" Detailed Activities

Each of the detailed activities under each stage of Plan, Do, and Review will be explained in the following sections.

PLAN

To improve the likelihood of success each project and each activity should be planned prior to doing it.

The output activities in the Plan stage are:

- Objectives
- Baseline
- Initial hypotheses
- REAL
- Approach
- Plan
- Reporting and stakeholders
- Preparation

1.1 - Objectives

The first step in running a project is to define the objectives of the project, which in turn answer the question of why you are doing the project in the first place.

For personal projects the objectives should include both the *outputs* of the projects and the *outcomes* that you seek to contribute to by doing the project. Project outputs are the tangible products, changes or goals that you seek from the project—which must be specific and measurable. For example, you may run a personal project to lose 20 pounds. The outcomes of the project reflect how you want your life to be as a result of doing the project. To continue the weight loss example, the outcomes you are seeking from losing weight are more energy, a more positive body image, improved health and so on.

Often the broader outcomes in life that support our vision will require a portfolio of several projects and ongoing actions to achieve them. It usually doesn't make sense to talk about a project for a good life—rather, a good life portfolio sets the right expectations about what will likely be involved in moving toward a better life, and maintaining that life after the projects are finished.

As you engage further with your project in the planning stage (and even when doing the project), you'll be able to get a better understanding of what you are trying to achieve, and thus be able to make your objectives more precise.

Nevertheless, it is essential at this stage to have an understanding of your personal burning platform for change. Projects can be hard, and you'll likely face setbacks before achieving your goal. By not having a clear and compelling reason to do the project at the start *and* writing this down, you risk forgetting why you're doing the project, and possibly give up when other parts of your life become more hectic.

Exercise 18.1—Your Project Objectives

You will write a short statement that sums up your project objectives. To help with this, answer the following questions.

- Why are you doing the project (i.e., your burning platform)?
- What does good look like from the perspective of the project?
- What are the three key things that the project will achieve?
- How will you know if the project is a success?

Write your project objectives statement now. You can write it as a paragraph or a series of bullet points.

1.2—Baseline

The best way to be able to see the changes that your project is making is to create a baseline or description of your personal "world" at project commencement. What I mean by world is a cross-section of thoughts, feelings, and measurements that are relevant to the project. For example, if your project is to lose 20 pounds, then your current world is not only your weight but also how you feel about that, the types of activities that you do or don't do as a result of the extra weight and so on. You could also take a photo or video of yourself. Many people who want to change jobs describe a feeling of the Sunday afternoon blues in anticipation of the coming workweek—that is part of the world that they inhabit. Other measures to include in the baseline at the start of your project are the values from 1 to 5 of your Five Pillar scores.

As I was coming off the road from my old job and sought to get fitter, I wrote out statements that concerned how I was feeling at the time. One thing that struck me was that being unfit not only reduced my energy level, but also made my thinking less clear. It also made me less open to trying new things.

A baseline is important to help you track progress and to give you the motivation to keep going if you become stuck in your project.

Exercise 18.2—Your Project Baseline

What are the key measures for your project?

How will you know if your project is successful?

Which time period should form the baseline for your project? Is it in the past, or today, or when you launch the project?

Record your baseline now.

1.3—Initial hypotheses

Often you may start a personal project not knowing what you want or the best approach to getting there.

Rather than get stuck in a cycle of rumination, it's often better to write down in several hypotheses what we think we're aiming to do and a possible approach to getting there. Each hypothesis is a statement about the problem or solution that we reasonably believe to be true, but don't yet *know* to be true. A hypothesis gives us permission to start, and a focus for our initial efforts. By having as a focus trying to find evidence to prove or disprove a hypothesis, we remain aware and learn from what we are experiencing, rather than letting whatever we learn slip away.

Let's use the example of a project to start a cupcake food truck. This project idea can be split into several hypotheses:

- That cupcakes are the best product to sell (Why: is there an unmet demand?)
- That a food truck is the best retail channel for your product

- That being self-employed will contribute to your overall standard of living (or at least be neutral) rather than detract from it

The discipline of trying to write down your hypotheses can often make visible some implicit but potentially incorrect assumptions with regard to your project idea, or, alternately, the real underlying reason that you want to do something. Perhaps the main appeal of starting a cupcake business is actually that you believe it will give you more freedom and flexibility than your current job. If so, then it's helpful to be aware of that assumption. It may not be true—many small business owners work longer hours than they did in their previous jobs, especially during the first few years after starting the business. If flexibility is your dominant need for a change of career, then you may find that there are other and better ways to do that rather than starting a business. You can start an exploratory project to find out.

Exercise 18.3–Your Project Hypotheses

Based on the objectives for the project, what are your hypotheses about the best approach to reach those objectives?

List yours hypotheses now.

1.4–REAL

Make your project REAL even before you start ramping it up. To remind you—REAL stands for Research, Engage, Analyze, and Learn. Complete a two-hour Internet research session on the parameters and scope of what you're trying to do. Place a special focus on reading about the approaches that other people in a situation similar to yours have used for a similar project.

Try to find a small action that you can take to experience part of the approach to the project, or one of the outcomes of the project.

Remember to analyze the outcomes of your efforts to ensure that you learn from this experience.

Throughout my professional career I've found that case studies of what other companies have done and how they did it are something that my clients really value. The research for your project might demonstrate that there are a broad range of people of all ages, life situations, and proficiency levels doing or trying to do the same thing as you. In addition to picking up tips and tricks on how to approach your project, it can be motivating to see that someone like you can make a change.

For almost any goal, a useful action that you could take to make it REAL is to write a short public blog or comment, or film yourself in a short video on the topic that you are seeking to engage in (even if you don't show that video to others). Your perspective for the writing or video could be, for example, a beginner's guide summarizing your research, or a personal story of your motivations and mindset for pursuing the goal. Even this simple exercise can switch your mindset from "receive" to "transmit", providing you with more insights and emotional progress than if you just thought about what you're trying to do.

Exercise 18.4—REAL

What is one concrete action that you can take in the next three days to make your project REAL?

Which of your key hypotheses can be tested using the REAL technique before firming up your project approach?

1.5—Approach

Next you must define the approach that you'll use to carry out your project. What are the key steps and stages that you must complete to make the project a reality? This activity is another great opportunity to engage others and ask them how they approached a similar goal, or to research this specific information online.

Most projects can be broken into logical stages or phases delineated by the production of an output, or by a change in the nature of the activities that will be performed after that point, or by a change in competency level. These delineation points are often called milestones.

Exercise 18.5–Your Project Approach

For your project, document the key steps that will be taken in order to reach your objective.

1.6–Plan

Based on your approach, you will create a draft plan for your project. The plan can simply be the list of activities against a timeline, or it can be an integrated document called a project charter, which I'll discuss in a moment. Your plan should, at a minimum, include several milestones and a timeline that is detailed enough so that it allows you to track your progress on a week-to-week basis.

If your project is more complex—for example, a project to start a business—then you may want to formally write up your planning steps in a document called a project charter. The project charter will contain a summary of why you're doing the project, the outcomes that you seek, relevant background to your project, the selected approach you intend follow, alternative approaches that you have investigated (in case you need to change or refine that approach later on), provisional milestones and a timeline. Often the creation of a project charter helps you to be clearer on what you're trying to achieve, and to identify linkages between different aspects of the project. It also allows you to have material on the project that can be shared with others so that you can get their feedback or other assistance.

Many project charters will also include some view of current issues (things that have already happened) and risks (things that may or may not happen) that you're aware of, and that may constitute obstacles to completing the project.

All project charters should include an evaluation of those key stakeholders affected by the project and a description of the proposed governance or accountability group, which is covered in the next activity.

Exercise 18.6–Your Project Plan

Draw up the timeline for your project.

If you believe that your project could benefit from a project charter then begin to draft it now.

1.7–Reporting and stakeholders

All projects should consider a review of stakeholders who will be affected by the project. In the case of personal projects it can be easy to become self-absorbed and forget that what you are seeking will undoubtedly affect others, including people close to you. Those stakeholders you identified in Chapter 6 may even see a project that you view as clearly positive in a negative light. This might be because it impacts them negatively, or because they haven't been through the learnings that you have. You will need to explain the project to them and "bring them along" to your level of understanding of what the project represents.

A special group of stakeholders are your accountability group, to whom you'll report project progress and look for support in completing your project.

Exercise 18.7–Your Project Stakeholders

Step 1—Identify stakeholders.

Identify the stakeholders. Use the list you created in Chapter 6 as a starting point.

Step 2—Identify impact.

For each of the key stakeholders, identify what impact the project will have on them—good, bad or neutral, from *their* perspective.

Step 3—Tailored response.

What would be an appropriate and tailored response to engage that stakeholder in what you are planning to do?

Step 4—Accountability group.

Who from your list of stakeholders will form your accountability group for the project?

Are there others from outside your immediate group who would/could be effective in helping to steer your project (e.g., mentors), if you were to engage them?

Step 5—Create stakeholder plan.

Document your plan for how and when you'll engage with the key stakeholders in your project. What actions must you take to address specific concerns your stakeholders may have? Which stakeholders must you bring along by sharing the objectives and progress of the project, and getting their feedback?

A step related to understanding the people aspects of your project is to define how you'll track and report the status of your project. Obviously, you are a key stakeholder in your project, and for project effectiveness I recommend tracking the status of the project at the same time every week, and producing some kind of written log of its status and your thoughts and actions to that point.

The purposes of status tracking on a personal project include:

- Measuring progress against project objectives and taking corrective actions where necessary
- Being proactive in managing risks and issues relating to your project before they derail the project completely
- Identifying areas where you need help with your project

At a minimum your project tracking should include an assessment of progress against tasks planned for the week just finished and a review of planned tasks for the week to come.

Exercise 18.8 – Your Project Reporting

Define your project reporting approach. When, how, and where will you track your project (and the status of your good life journey).

1.8 – Preparation

Preparation is a planning activity that you can start even if you don't know specifically what your project is and how it will work.

You can prepare financially by ensuring that you have access to the funds required to complete your project. If your project involves time off work or a reduced income, then the common advice I received was to try to put aside 6-12 months' salary in advance to support this. For many of you this might sound impossible (which doesn't make the advice untrue). Nevertheless, as I described with the offsetting concept, we often manage to find money to spend to make ourselves feel better about any pain in our lives. This could be shopping, or vacations, or time at the pub and so on. Creating a project may provide you with just enough of a reason to begin to funnel these offsetting funds into a bank account, or at least to postpone increasing your discretionary financial commitments until your future path becomes clearer.

Remember though that the most effective approach to a change involving your work (and often a financial necessity) is to use experiments and even a side business while keeping your main source of income from a current job. In some cases you'll want to involve the organization that you currently work with in the project directly. For example, if your personal project includes skills-based volunteering or other areas where work and personal value overlap, then you may be able to negotiate the inclusion of the project in your normal working hours, or even as part of your work goals.

DO

The Do stage of your project may take days, weeks, or even years. Even so, this doesn't mean that you start the Do stage and never look at or change the project until it finally succeeds. Instead you go through a mini-cycle of plan, do, review for each activity or group of activities. Once you begin executing the plan that you've created, you'll also begin to make progress and/or get feedback that will require corrective action to keep your project on track.

A project is usually more difficult and takes longer than we originally anticipate. Although planning will increase your chance of success, it is also important to know that many personal projects go through a cycle or several cycles of optimism, reality, disillusionment, and then progress.

Knowing this in advance can help to increase the chance of success for your project, since "forewarned is forearmed."

We typically start a project with high expectations (otherwise why would we do it in the first place?) and are bolstered by some quick initial progress toward our goal. Then we encounter setbacks. Setbacks are a normal part of achieving anything worthwhile. At work we tend to be able to find the resolve to push through setbacks, while in personal change initial setbacks can stop a project in its tracks. The reason is that we begin to feel disillusionment, which I think all of us can agree is a negative feeling. Doing a personal project is supposed to make us feel good, and when it doesn't we suddenly want to stop doing it, rather than recognizing that disillusionment is a step toward progress. We rid ourselves of disillusionment by sticking with our plan, reminding ourselves of the burning platform for the project, and tenaciously seeking a way around obstacles.

Even when we are progressing, things usually take longer than we expect, which also doesn't feel good. Then we're in danger of seeking other activities that give us a shorter-term hit of good feeling. The way to avoid getting side-tracked in your project is to celebrate small wins, particularly at the start. This is the psychology of positive reinforcement. For example, as I continued to ride laps around the lake near my house I'd reward myself by having an extra breakfast taco the first time I added one or more 10-mile laps to what my prior maximum was. The celebration doesn't have to be big, and often it's better if it isn't, so that it doesn't give you such a good feeling that you stop doing the project! Save your big celebration for the end, but do celebrate small wins.

The activities for the Do phase are:

2.1 Action cycle

2.2 Progress tracking

2.3 Accountability group

2.4 Transition

2.1–Action cycle

The core of the Do cycle will look different from project to project depending on the nature of the project. The activities involved in starting a charity will look different from those involved in a project to climb Mount Everest. What won't change is that you should still use the plan, do, review cycle for each of the actions and steps that you take. Think about *what am I trying to achieve with this step*? Then do the step and measure the outcome.

Keeping the discipline of the plan, do, review cycle as you execute project steps will help to keep your mind engaged in ensuring that each of the smaller actions contribute to what you are trying to achieve overall. This is particularly relevant, since many of you will be doing your personal project in small fragments of time—a few minutes here, an hour there.

Often, taking any action at all will generate further actions or ideas and possible new directions. Ensure that you have some way to track and categorize these ideas and actions as you go along. This means that you won't lose the ideas, and you can also prevent them from distracting you.

The review stage of your action cycle is the place where you decide what the implication of these new ideas or directions is. Are they relevant to your project, or should they be saved for later, or perhaps just ignored while you focus on the key objectives of your project?

Remember the discipline of directing energy. Many project actions, although important, can be done during a period of lower quality energy and time, rather than at a time of peak concentration. For example, an action that involves Internet research could be done when you're on the phone, or at other times when you would otherwise be mindlessly trawling the Internet or reviewing social media.

Using a project to achieve a goal means that you should always know what the next immediate and highest priority action to achieve your goal is. It's amazing how quickly small fragments of time, if used in a focused way, can translate into real progress toward your goal.

2.2–Progress tracking

All projects should be tracked on a periodic basis to ensure that they remain on target to achieve the objectives you set for them. For most projects a weekly tracking cycle works the best (as I've said before). Projects will vary in intensity and effort required over the course of the project. If there is a lot happening at some point in your project you may wish to take the additional step of creating a daily plan and tracking progress each day.

Even if at times you need daily tracking on your project, it still makes sense to have a weekly cycle to sum up progress against your plan, to consider risks to your project's success, and to prompt you to identify areas where you may require additional help.

For projects that will take longer than three months to complete I recommend adding an agenda point every month to review your progress against the project charter that you created at the start. It's likely that longer projects will also be more complex, and this often means that you'll understand what you're trying to do, why you're doing it, and the best way to do it much better as you proceed. These monthly checkpoints provide you an opportunity to refine your approach to the project, ensuring that you get the most out of it and in the most efficient way. They also provide an opportunity to engage your accountability group.

As you reach approximately the last third of your project you'll want to add an agenda item in your weekly and monthly reviews to consider the transition activity, which will be discussed later in this chapter.

2.3–Accountability group

When you planned your project you identified a special group of stakeholders that will form your accountability group.

The planning phase of a project can take much longer than expected. This is not due to the amount of physical work to be done, but simply because by its nature planning involves iteration and reflection, and also finding the right motivation and time to start.

Given this, it's important that you maintain contact with your accountability group on a periodic basis. Ensure that you communicate with the group ahead of the firm start date of the Do phase of the project, and at that time confirm what's expected from them in the accountability group relationship.

The simplest example of an accountability group is a friend that you decide to accompany to the gym. A bigger group might include mentors, specialists, and other advisors, and be split into different subgroups that you meet with in different cycles of the project and discuss various topics with.

The minimum qualification for an accountability group member is that they can be honest with you, and better if they are can also maintain a level of arms-length detachment from you and the project. Honesty is a two-way street, requiring that you communicate honestly the whats and whys of your project, and that you give that person permission to give you "tough love" before you ask them to be honest.

Although your friends and family are obvious candidates for your accountability group, they may not always be objective about your project, given how it may impact them. Sometimes having a more arms-length relationship with an accountability group member who can also offer assistance and expert feedback on your project works best.

2.4—Transition

The final steps in the Do phase of a project concern consolidation of what you've done on the project and transition to life after the project has finished.

The transition activity is about more than simply tying up loose ends. This activity concerns what you put in place after the project is finished.

As you progress through your project there should come a point where you see clearly for the first time, understanding the true nature of what you are doing. In practical terms this means you can see which actions lead to positive outcomes, and which are neutral or destructive.

Once you really understand what elements (habits, practices) of the project have affected your life in a positive way, you must design your philosophy, process, and practice of living to support these same elements once the project is over. This may be as simple as ensuring that you continue the new habits that you've started, or at least continue to follow them in a modified way.

For example, if your project to lose 20 pounds was successful and you've lost the weight, then what do you do next week? Instead of going to the gym five times a week, maybe you'll go just three times. Instead of a severe diet you may transition to simpler principles of eating that will provide nutrition but not further weight loss.

Other wrapping-up activities could include consolidation and backing up (where applicable) any notes or materials that you've used on the project.

REVIEW

The nature of personal projects is that the outcomes we seek from such projects are rarely sustained automatically after the project is finished.

For example, you may choose to start a personal project to run a marathon. Apart from completing the race, it's likely that there will be other outcomes that you sought from the marathon, such as becoming fitter or feeling a sense of achievement. Being fit and living a good life is the result of a process rather than a one-shot effort. With many projects there is the risk that we lose the progress we've made, or even backtrack when the project wraps up. One reason for this is that we begin to focus on other areas, and stop doing the things that made our project a success. The Review phase aims to enable you to sustain the benefits from the work you've put in after the Do phase is completed.

The activities for the Review phase are:

- Progress assessment
- Extend/continuous improvement
- Lessons learned
- Help someone

3.1–Progress Assessment

When the project is completed you'll want to complete a post-project assessment, measuring against the original objectives for the project. The best time for this is one, two, or three months after the project has finished. I recommend waiting three months or 100 days after the project has been completed before doing the review. This provides enough time to see the true results of the project, and also for any "teething" issues to be resolved.

3.2–Extend/Continuous improvement

Often the best way to maintain the major benefits of a project is to put into place a process to seek other incremental benefits over time. This works by maintaining focus and a measurement mindset concerning the topic area of the project.

You'll also be in a better position now to identify how to extend the benefits of the project, either by running a future project or through further actions. By having taken action, it's likely that you'll now see the world in a different way. New possibilities and permutations on what you've just done will become visible. Remember to record these thoughts and add them to your project file. You should do this even if you intend to continue working on your project straight away. Sometimes things change, and if you don't pick up the project for a while you'll risk losing your ideas if you haven't written them down.

3.3–Lessons Learned

It's likely that you'll run a series of small and larger projects over your lifetime. Completing a project means that you learn more about the subject matter, you learn more about yourself, and you learn more about the process of doing projects.

All of these insights should be captured in order to crystallize the learning you've gained and to help you in future.

Part of enabling your future growth is creating an environment in which, over time, the ability to initiate change becomes easier. Not that the effort involved in performing the steps required to effect change will be less, but your expectations about the nature of personal change will have adjusted to be more honest and open. You will come to recognize the nature of challenge and change and also welcome it, as with an old friend or adversary. Use an action in any part of your life as evidence supporting further action. Even if you tried something in one part of life and it didn't work, having a project mindset reduces the likelihood that you'll give up trying to make changes in future.

Lessons learned can also be communicated to others who are attempting a similar type of project.

3.4–Help Someone

Another great way to consolidate the benefits of your project is to help someone else. You could mentor someone or share your lessons learned, or offer to participate in an accountability group. There is a saying that when we teach, we learn twice.

We sometimes look around the world in search of an opportunity to make a contribution, and to find meaning. Why not use your trials and experiences as material to build a platform that helps others live a good life more quickly and effectively?

Helping someone else is a great way to pay forward the benefits of your change, and to help create an environment that encourages others to become helpers, too.

Exercise 18.9–Helping Someone

Identify one person who could benefit from your experience in a personal project that you ran.

Make a plan to engage that person within the next month. If you haven't found a person to help, then write a short blog post explaining what you did and what you learned.

∽ ∽ ∽

As you finish your project, it would be timely to review your pillars again and your DEEP portfolio of changes. You may feel energized and ready to take on the next phase of your project; if so, that's great. Remember that your project will likely have unlocked new possibilities that you couldn't see before. Your next ROLE project may be in a different pillar. It might be to make a larger contribution by taking what you've done and learned to a wider audience. Celebrate your success and take a moment to see the possibilities in front of you.

NOTES

CHAPTER 19
Place

Before concluding this book I'd like to talk briefly about *place*, which instead of being a pillar in its own right provides the context within which the other pillars operate. It can also play a critical role in defining the quality of your life experience.

It's not too simplistic to say that if we shuttle between the same places by the same routes every day, then that is the definition of a rut. Some places let us think creatively and expansively; others curb our creativity and create stress. Unfortunately, many of the work environments that we spend so much time in fall into the latter category.

In this chapter I'd like you to think about what places you'd like to live and work in, or visit. Places that you need in your life in order to get the most out of it.

Often we try to do *new* thinking in an *old* place—a place associated with our present situation and past ways of thinking. Where are you reading this book? Is the place helping or hindering you toward expansive and unconstrained thinking about your future? What role is place playing in the current scores that you've assigned to your pillars or the future opportunities that you've identified?

As someone who has travelled around the world many times, I can say that we don't need to go on holiday to open our minds. Vacations can be great, though cost and maintaining that same mindset when we come back home can be difficult. And although we can do "big picture" thinking on holiday, we rarely force ourselves to get into the necessary details, including the concrete actions that need to be taken. Even if we become motivated at the time, it can be difficult to take action from your deck chair on the other side of the world.

Instead of going on holiday to change your life (or at least after you get back!), I'd suggest finding a space in the city where you live or work, though not a place that is part of your normal routine. This may be a coffee shop, the local library, or a park. If you work in an office block it could be a vacant office on a different floor. If you've read this book through in one go and intend to go back to do the exercises or plan an experiment or project, then do your second reading of the book in this new place.

Use the space to reflect and think exclusively about the Good Life and your personal projects. Try to do this thinking when you're not too tired, i.e., don't leave this important task until the last thing before bed. Why not try to adjust your start or finish times at work so that you can allocate some peak concentration time in the office to the most important tasks across all pillars of your life?

Most of all, be flexible by being prepared. Keep your copy of *The Good Life Book* (or a notepad or electronic device) on hand, and get in the habit of using it when inspiration strikes, wherever you may be at the time.

CONCLUSION

Congratulations on reaching the end of the book. Each of the 19 chapters that you've read contains one or more essential skills that represent both a step on your good life journey and an ability that you can re-use to maintain a good life in future. Remember to complete the exercises, then use REAL and DEEP to take action!

Let me close with one final lesson. The Good Life is simply life. It is an attempt to wrestle that challenge thrown down to all of us at birth concerning what to do with our time on the planet. Don't let a good life become another thing you become attached to attaining and possessing. A good life is not a thing—it is who you are.

I hope that you've found some truth—your truth—from completing this book. As professionals we can fight a million battles in our minds before the first shot is ever fired in practice. I hope that, if nothing else, the time spent with this book has energized your mind enough so that you can take action toward living a good life in weeks rather than years or decades, or not at all.

Be a leader. Create a movement for positive change in your own life and beyond. Do it *before* you have enough courage, enough skills, and enough time. The perfect time doesn't exist and never will.

This is the final stage of your evolution to a good life, where you take everything you've learned in this book and apply it, making a positive change in the world.

What the world needs now is *you*.

Good luck on your journey and may it be a good one!

IN MEMORIAM

Brian Richard Cowell (1946-2017)

My Dad

For speaking, coaching and media inquiries, please contact:

Brett Cowell

www.brettcowell.com
media@totallifecomplete.com
Twitter: @brettcowelltw

INDEX

A

Actions for Pillars, 76, 84, 90, 95, 101, 105
Agape, 151
Art of Seeing, 116-120
    Focus, 116
    Openness, 120
    Viewpoint, 116-120
Assumptions, 118, 121, 123, 126, 193, 213
Authenticity, 34, 99

B

Balanced Life, 18, 132
Baseline, 49, 209, 211-212
Basic Productivity System, 53
Benefits of a Good Life, 58
Big-Bang Type, 30
Bringing Love, 153
Burning Platform, 50, 57-59, 126, 189, 210-211, 220
Burning Platform Statement, 59
Business Social Value, 175, 178-179

C

Calibration Process, 75
Career, 27, 29, 45-46, 61, 69-70, 77, 81, 98, 114, 122, 124-125, 130-133, 145, 157, 163, 174, 192, 213-214
Challenges, 77, 93-94, 98, 112, 158, 192
Character Traits, 34, 37, 65, 71, 103, 126, 162
Choices Strategic, 115, 121
Circles Exercise, 30-31, 33, 42, 52
Comfort Zone, 35-36, 98, 137, 144, 156-158, 181, 192
Common Problems, 71, 145, 157
Community Engagement,175, 180
Concept of Potential, 126
Concrete actions, 54, 56, 104, 230
Consciousness, 91-92, 137-138, 170
Consumption Activities, 97, 101
Core Beliefs, 37-38, 64,117-118
Core Skills, 68, 70
Core Values, 33
Creating a Vision, 10, 45
Creating Value, 162
Croatia, 164
Current Life Score, 50-51
Cycle of Life, 188
Cycle of Self-Reflection, 39

D

Defining Characteristic, 26, 51, 89
Demonstrated Values, 162
Descriptions for Good, 74, 83, 89, 94, 100
Directing Energy, 20-21, 103, 188, 221
Do Phase, 220-225
    Accountability Group, 221, 223-224
    Action Cycle, 220-222
    Progress Tracking, 220, 222-223
    Transition, 221, 224

E

Emotional and Financial Investment, 30
Enabling Growth, 20, 188
Escaping the Bubble, 144
Experiments, 29-30, 42, 63, 79, 114, 118-119, 133, 188, 191-197, 199-200, 205, 219, 230
Expression Pillar, 82, 97, 99-101
External Obstacles, 131

F

Financial and Non-Financial Returns, 69, 125
Financial Value, 62, 65-66, 72-73, 125
Financials, 55-56
    Conclusions, 56
    Financial Information, 55-56
    Group Spending Into Categories, 55
Finding Courage, 155
Five Minds, 136-142
    Classic Mind, 136, 139
    Ego Mind, 136, 140
    Hidden Mind, 136, 141-142
    Primitive Mind, 136, 138-139
    Universal Mind, 136-137, 140
Five Pillars, 34, 44, 59, 62-63, 93, 103, 105-106, 116, 122, 133, 164, 200
    Expression, 62, 97-101
    Health, 62, 85-90
    People, 62, 77-84
    Spirit, 62, 91-95
    Vocation, 62-76
Five Whys Technique, 35-39
Focus, 116, 128, 132, 157
Freedom, 7, 28, 88, 155, 159-161, 163, 213
Future Direction, 31, 105
Future Vision, 19, 45

G

Global Financial Crisis, 146
Good Life Journey, 10, 13, 17, 20-23, 30, 38, 42, 57, 63, 92, 103, 106, 111, 116, 187, 192, 218, 231
Good Life, Definition, 20, 62, 190

H

Habits, 17, 54, 106, 115-116, 131, 137, 156, 196, 224
Happiness, 16, 45, 66, 86, 118, 145-146, 155, 159-160, 164-167, 193
Health Pillar, 88-90
Healthy Spiritual State, 93
Holistic State of Living, 18
Hong Kong, 92
Hope, 18, 21, 34, 43, 45, 55, 58, 81, 94, 112-113, 126, 128, 132, 144, 165-166, 181, 185, 188, 231
Hypothesis, 194, 209, 212-214

I

Imaginary Job Description, 24-25
Imaginary Meeting, 138-140
Immersion, 147, 152-153
Important Aspects of Life, 61
Impressions, 22
Improved Significance, 18
Improving Lives, 82
Informal Research, 75, 84
Initial Journey, 20, 188
Initial Observations, 22
Intellectual Assets, 71-72, 75
Internal Obstacles, 131, 189, 191
Intrinsic Happiness, 164, 166-167

J-K

Journey, 4
Key Characteristics, 73-75, 82-83, 88-89, 94, 99
Key Decisions, 114, 189-191
Key Elements, 46, 121
Keywords, 130

L

Languages Describing a Good
    Life, 15-22
    Attainment, 16-22
    Being, 16-22
    Gratification, 16-22
    Importance, 16-22
    Meaning, 16-22
Level of Vagueness, 46
Life Changes, 30
Life Opportunity Areas, 202
Life's Lessons, 113
Lifeline Activity, 36
Lifeline Exercise, 31, 88, 171
Lifestyle, 43, 55-57, 64, 123, 127, 129, 132-133, 143, 150, 161
List of Passions, 42
Location Independent, 45, 72, 75, 81
London, 28, 43, 68, 87, 143
Long-Term Impact, 191

M

Making Decisions, 118, 122, 189
Managing Time, 20
Meeting of Minds, 136
Mentoring Others, 174, 176
Minimum Viable Product (MVP), 71
Model Practices, 75, 84, 90, 95, 100

Moving Jobs, 69-70
Music, 27-28, 30, 98

N

Neutral Facilitator, 136
New York, 80, 112, 145
Non-Financial Value, 62, 65-66, 73, 125
North Star, 18
Nurturing Connection, 135, 146

O-P

Offsetting, 54, 56, 64, 219
Pareto, 67, 78
Part One Summary, 104
Passion, 23-24, 26, 29, 31, 35, 42-44, 46, 65, 69, 72, 103, 106
Path of Attainment and Gratification, 17
Peace of Mind, 56, 151, 155-156
Perception of Happiness, 86
Perfectionism, 140, 170
Personal Expression, 18, 30
Personal Flair, 186
Personal Introduction, 52
Personal System, 139
Personal Transformation, 146
Physical Domain, 86
Physical Training, 86
Plan Phase, 209-219
    Approach, 214-215
    Baseline, 211-212
    Initial Hypotheses, 212-213
    Objectives, 210-211
    Plan, 215-216
    Preparation, 218-219
    Real, 213-214
    Reporting and Stakeholders, 216-218

Plan, Do, Review technique, 208-209
Plane of possibilities, 113, 120
Poetry, 87, 100, 169, 185
Porsche, 45-46
Positive Effects, 100, 175
Positive Work Environment, 174, 176
Problem-Solving Skills, 68
Productive Belief, 118
Professional Bubble, 135, 142
Professional Careers, 124, 131-132
Professional Life, 149-150
Professionalism, 70
Project Management, 67, 70, 77, 197, 208
Project Outputs, 198, 202, 210
Project Reporting, 218
Provisional Timeline, 203
Purpose, 43-44

Q-R

Quality Energy, 80, 221
Real me, 111, 128, 130-131
Real Self, 23
REAL technique, 203-205
Removal of Obstacles, 21
Resourceful Execution, 21
Review Phase, 225-227
    Continuous Improvement, 226
    Helping Someone, 227
    Lessons Learned, 226-227
    Progress Assessment, 225
Rocket Ship, 17, 42
Role-Modeling, 20, 176
Routines, 106

S

Scarcity Example, 120
Self-Awareness, 133, 146
Self-Concept, 64, 128-129
Self-Help Gurus, 45
Self-Insights, 105
Self-Talk, 142, 148
Serenity Prayer, 156
Seven Loves, 147-153
    Awe and Wonder, 152
    Expression and Immersion, 152-153
    Love of Friends and Family, 147
    Love of God, 151-152
    Self-Love, 147-149
    Selfless Love, 150-151
    Sexual Love, 149-150
Single Defining Characteristic, 51
Skills-Based Volunteering, 42, 70, 175, 177-178, 180, 219
Social Entrepreneurship, 173, 175, 179-180
Social Involvement, 175, 180
Societal Aspects, 159
Sources of Happiness, 165-166
Specialization of Knowledge in, 132
Spirit Pillar, 91, 93-95
Stakeholder List, 79-80
Stakeholder Management, 77-82
    Awareness, 78
    Monitoring, 79
    Tailored Response, 79
Starting a Business, 28, 71, 213
Subconscious mind, 23, 45, 73
Success, 16-19, 72, 77-78, 80, 111, 115, 118, 126-128, 133-134, 148, 160, 165, 167, 173, 179, 186, 188, 195-198, 205, 209, 211, 219-220, 222, 225, 228
Success Trap, 115, 126
Supporting Disciplines, 20, 103, 111, 188, 221

Sustained Happiness, 159, 165-166

T

Tenacity, 29, 34, 112, 179
Thinking, 16-17, 29, 65, 69, 71, 91-92, 97, 104, 112, 118, 120-121, 123, 129, 134-136, 138-142, 149, 174, 195, 204, 211, 229-230
Thomas Edison, 29
Three Stages for a Good Life,
    Getting There, 183, 186, 212
    Starting Your Good Life Journey, 13, 22, 103
    Staying on Track, 109, 111
Time Audit, 53-54
Transformational Journey, 148
Turning Point, 18, 32-33
Typical Week, 144, 167

U

Unconstrained Vision, 21, 41
Understand Who You Are,
    Four Exercises, 23-39
    Core Beliefs, 38-39
    Core Values, 34-38
    Lifeline, 31-34
    Three Circles, 23-31
Understanding Sensitivity, 73, 83, 89, 94, 99
Unlocking Potential, 20, 111, 188
    Connection, 111-114
    Contribution, 111, 114
    Courage, 111, 113-114
    Humor, 111, 113-114
    Perspective, 111, 113-114

V

Viewpoint Changes, 201
Viewpoints, 17, 117-118
    Born or Made, 117
    Chaos or Order, 117
    Fear or Promise, 117
    Have or Be, 117
    Industrial or Organic, 117
    Job or Portfolio, 117
    Man or Nature, 117
    Scarcity or Abundance, 117, 119
    Self or Others, 117
    Thing or Process, 117
Vision, 16, 19, 21, 41-47, 56, 61-64, 72-73, 81-82, 88, 93, 99, 103-106, 111-112, 116, 141, 146, 149, 181, 186, 189, 210
Vision for Expression, 99
Vision for Health, 88
Vision for People, 81-82
Vision for Spirit, 93
Vision for Vocation, 73
Visualization, 44-45, 86
Vocation Pillar, 63, 65, 73-74, 76, 81
Vocational Portfolio, 26, 65-66, 70-72, 74-75, 124-126, 187, 193
Volunteering, 42, 68, 70, 173-175, 177-178, 180, 219

W

What does good look like?, 19-20
Work me, 111, 127-128, 130
Work Self, 23
Work/life balance, 61

NOTES

NOTES

www.ingramcontent.com/pod-product-compliance
Lightning Source LLC
Chambersburg PA
CBHW050532300426
44113CB00012B/2052